Disciple of a
Master

How to Hit a Baseball to Your Potential

by Stephen J. Ferroli
foreword by Ted Williams

Design: Greg Wood
Photographs: Charles Bradford
Diagrams: Ken Dickinson

ACKNOWLEDGEMENTS

Special Thanks to:
(at random)

Jane Mathieson
Ma, Dads, Rick and Bink
Charles Bradford
Greg Wood
Ken Dickinson
Jack Edwards
Mr. & Mrs. James Edwards
Adam Frattasio
John Frattasio
Devine & Partners, Inc.
Harold Walsh, ATI
Harry Hood, F. P. Inc.
Carolyn Philippon
Jan Ostrum
Mary McDonagh
Stephen Greene
Diane Fernald
The Davies
The Burkes
Bill Cook
Dr. Pamela Gray
Dr. Marilyn Cairns
Hanover Jr. High
Hanover High School
Darrel Brandon
Ron C. Duke
Fred Doll
Mike Farrel
Bill Wilcox
Fred Brown
Robert Condon
Dan Mannis
Dr. Lawrence Kleine
Peter A. Adams

Charles King
Earl Matheson
T.W.C. Staffs and Campers
Peggy Farrel/W.W.
Frank Niles
James Sylvia
Hank Kowalski
Robert Norton
Prof. Anne Coakley
Dr. Edward Braun
Scott Mottau
Ross Mottau
Bill Adams
The Captain
Buck Smith
Shorty
The Wakas Kid
Barry Parker (Babo)
Rick Ide
Mark Luddy
Larry Patch
Timbone
Donna Mazzamurro
Bridgewater State College
Mr. James Mahoney
Industrial Photographic Services
Beatrice Anne Mottau
Bernie
Kate
Andy, Doc, Bud and Sweets
Goona
All the Coaches and teams I've played for.

Published by Line Drive Publishing
113 Pleasant Street
Hanover, MA 02339

Library of Congress Registration
Number TXU 209 575

ISBN: 0-939905-00-0

To Ted, and all the young baseball players of America,
who dream, as I did, of becoming great hitters.
May this help you even a wee bit more.

PREFACE

Before we even start, let's get a few things straight. 1) I am not a writer, an editor, or a copy editor. What I am is a student and teacher of hitting baseballs. In this book, however, to at least some degree, I have worn all those hats; and therefore, I must warn you. Literary mayhem is not only likely but probable. 2) Due to the complexity of what I'm about to say in relation to where the skill of hitting stands today, I want you to know that I knew years ahead of time that this book would *not* head baseball's best seller list. Fearing the possibility of its shelf death in the cold hands of big business, while at the same time understanding the importance of what it could mean to the game, I decided to maintain a good portion of it's control and publish it with a small group of investors. Hence, *Line Drive Publishing*. I feel that by taking this route, I will always have the peace of mind in knowing that this book was originally judged on its *merit* as opposed to its position on a sales graph. Finally, due to a lack of finance, this book is not a dress-up affair. If you're looking for sparkle and flash, you're in the wrong place. Here, it's just me, wearing the clothes that I had clean, preaching *what* I believe and *why* I believe it.

In closing, I would like you to be aware of the blank "note pages" located at the back of the book. If *learning* is the goal, I don't think anyone should read anything without a pencil on hand.

INTRODUCTION

Ted had dreamed, and I knew that; but dreaming never seemed as important as it did that day. He had reviewed my work — work on the subject that he continues to spend his life analyzing from every angle. Now he had requested to see me; this was it. He was the Number One Man, and I knew my ideas could go no higher. I'll never forget that day. My anticipation, followed by the compliment of his approval, encouragement and support, added up to be the thrill of my life. Reliving that day, however, one element has become far more impressive than its adventure or excitement. Standing immortally above this man's impeccable history of production was his way of *thinking,* his *judgment,* and his *values.* This man cared; he listened, and he was patient. His attitude was one of *moving forward.* To this man, dreaming was trying and doing. He hadn't sat back and merely hoped, he had identified his dream and sought it with heart, mind and soul. He was a great man. From that day on, it all became so clear, regardless of whether or not a person gets to live their dream, it is the "dreaming" — the relentless pursuit of a distant desire — that is the only stage for a man's or woman's greatest effort. Now I both understand and respect it, for it was dreaming that had made this man, and it was dreaming that had brought me before him.

FOREWORD

It really doesn't seem that long since that cold, drizzling, doghouse day when I stepped to the plate in Fenway Park for my last at bat as a Red Sox player. And today, between casts or while cruising the Florida waters, often I'll find time to vividly rerun that last "at bat" or one of the many other fine memories of my career in professional baseball.

But you know, I've got to laugh because while my statistics will show a wide assortment of highlights to look back on, the memories that have become my fondest are those which feature an "effort" more so than a highlight — an effort not only of mine, but many times of someone else's who tried with me or cared for me and therefore contributed toward transforming those No. 9 highlights from mere dreams to realities.

Much like those memories, when I first met and talked with Steve Ferroli, I could tell that he had put forth a serious effort toward understanding and helping the skill of hitting. Not only had this young New England hitter practiced his way to potential by learning the do's and don'ts of good hitting in the cage and on the field, but also in college as a physical education major, he had come to understand the scientific principles behind the skill as well. After several discussions, it became evident that Steve knew much more about hitting than most people will ever know on this subject. Naturally, I took an interest in him.

With this rare breed of knowledge formed through unbiased hitting experience and academics, Steve then began to analyze the theories and teaching procedures that produce the hitters in baseball today. Steve's findings, along with his care for the skill's future, led him to write this book, where he has done a spectacular job, not only defending my theory of hitting against others, illustrating and explaining the pros and cons involved, but also where he has extended upon my theory, making it stronger and more effective for the future.

Ted Williams

CONTENTS

Ted Williams: A Lost Model Of Execution

Looking back, it's kind of funny because when I was in grade school the name "Ted Williams" was an aggravation to me. His endorsement of several Sears & Roebuck sporting products had placed his autograph on what seemed to be everything; bats, gloves, weights, tents, fishing rods — everything! In Sears his name was almost as famous as the little "r" with the circle around it. Couple that kind of autograph exposure with endless stories from my grandmother about how "that Williams" had disgraced baseball by spitting and swearing at those who loved him . . . and in no time at all I had developed a "Williams Swilliams" attitude.

It didn't seem long before my personal quest in hitting led me to the top floor of "The John Curtis Free Library" in my hometown of Hanover, Massachusetts. It was there I stood a high school ballplayer; all heart, dreams, and desire; and it was there that it all started. Not only did I then begin to pay a long string of overdue notices on *The Science of Hitting*, a 97-page classic written by, of all people, Ted Williams, but I also began an endless study of the hardest single act in the sporting world. Much like the Atlantic Salmon, I was hooked for life.

I think everyone gets their calling, and I heard mine when I realized how little the game of baseball knew about hitting 14 years after Williams' book. Though you probably don't realize it, hitters today are far below their potential; and I'm talking from professional baseball right down the line. Believe me, the quality of this skill's teaching and study has declined with its statistics. As a result, hitters today don't know what to do, when to do it, or why to do it; and each spring illogical instruction continues to be fed to millions of young hitters from positions of trust, respect, and authority.

While my ultimate goal is to help solve the problems in hitting today, I know that goal can only be reached after "the hitting world" — that is, anyone who hits, teaches, or talks the skill — decides to approach the art with "logic." Unfortunately, in the past I have found hitting discussion to be anything but logical. For example, a quick peek at Ted's career portrays him something like this: Named to Baseball's Hall of Fame in 1966 — last of the .400 hitters, hit .406 in 1941 —

American League batting champion six times, home run champion four times, led American League in total bases six times, in bases on balls eight times, in slugging percentage nine times — American League MVP in 1946 and 1949 and hit .304 in 16 All-Star games.

It is obvious from these statistics that Ted Williams was awesome. Now consider he had only average speed and lost five years in his prime to military service, and there is no doubt we are talking about possibly the greatest hitter who ever lived. Yet, despite Ted's credibility, it is interesting to note how quick the logic of today has labeled his approach to hitting as one that is unrealistic for the *average young hitter* to learn or use. The tendency has become to call Ted a natural hitter — to cast him off as a *talent phenomenon*. I hear this "natural hitter pitch" thrown at Williams all the time and I think it's ridiculous. *Ted Williams was not a talent phenomenon*. Granted, the man did have good eyesight; however, physically, as a hitter many have been much faster and stronger with equal vision and smaller strike zones. Certainly, he was not more fortunate than, say, Pete Rose or George Brett. However, when their careers are over, they won't have compiled the all-around stats of Williams. Why is that?

Ted Williams signed as a pitcher with San Diego *standing 6'3" and weighing 148 pounds*. What did Williams think when he looked in the mirror? It couldn't have mattered much because in the next three years he would become one of the best hitters in the American Association; hits, home runs, R.B.I.'s, everything. Remember: 6'3", 148 pounds! Where did his power come from?

In his younger years Ted Williams grew up in San Diego, California which was, as he would say, "a place where a kid could stretch the baseball season to the depths of his imagination." While the California sun certainly played its role in his success, it's interesting to note that as a kid, Ted felt there were two boys in his neighborhood that were better than he was. Now, if you think about that for a minute, couldn't we assume that there is at least one kid in every neighborhood in the rest of California and in the rest of the country that had Williams' potential? Where does all this talent go?

I would think one of the most important peo-

2

ple in Williams' life was Roger Hornsby (lifetime average .358, HR 302). Williams felt that Hornsby knew what it took to be a good hitter. So as a kid, looking up to Hornsby, Williams would constantly ask him questions, hoping to gather information that he could use to improve himself. One of the best hitting statements I've ever heard was one that Hornsby told Williams many years ago. Hornsby would say, *Great hitters aren't born; they're made. They're made out of practice, fault-correction, and confidence.* Hopefully the point becomes clear, possibly the greatest hitter that ever lived was a tall, skinny kid with as many doubts and worries as any other. But despite his slender frame, through analysis and practice, driven by a burning desire to succeed, Ted learned to hit in such a way that presented the full extent of his ability. Remember, we're talking about a guy who *practiced until the blisters bled.* This man *worked* his way to potential; and it just so happened that when his abilities were used to their fullest, he was great. Physically speaking, Ted did not have the abilities that one would normally associate with being a great. How many tall, skinny kids do they sign today? What I want you to see is that Ted was a model of *execution*; and luckily for us, unlike genetics, execution can be worked upon.

The questions that arise over a tall skinny kid's success, where the missing talent goes, and why other greats statistically lag behind are formulated from a lack of hitting knowledge. Baseball does not understand how successful hitting is pieced together. Think about it. Why couldn't Danny Ainge hit in the major leagues? Any man that walks from the Toronto Blue Jays' infield onto the back court of the Boston Celtics has his share of ability. Why all the problems? Danny Ainge had trouble because he didn't execute properly. It's not that he couldn't have hit; it's that he didn't understand how. Ainge could have been a fine hitter. The point being that it is not just ability! (Please may this echo through each line to come.) What brings one to potential is ability alongside of good execution. Due to the fact that Danny's obvious talents were stripped away when the task became putting a bat on a ball, I feel his career becomes an ideal case study reflecting the important relation between one's ability and how it is perceived

through the quality of their execution. Putting it a little differently I could list you 50 hitters in the big time right now that couldn't wear Danny's sneaks in the talent department. However, all 50 would be better hitters due to the quality of their execution.

These people that are quick to place a stripe of superiority on Williams' shoulder are merely finding a convenient way to explain and deal with his greatness. While I can both understand and sympathize with how and why this lack of hitting knowledge has come about (I'll elaborate), the fact remains that these people are unknowingly and ironically restraining the finest theory of hitting ever recorded. It's time to wake up.

As I take my shot at opening your eyes, please keep in mind one important factor; I didn't write this book because Ted was my hero or idol. I never saw him play, not once. To me Ted Williams wasn't really a star, he was only a legend. I mean, I never saw him on TV. He wasn't a Yaz, Rose, Kaline, or Aaron; or for a kid today, maybe a Boggs, Brett, Cooper, or Clark. He was older — in black and white. This cowboy wasn't a Clint Eastwood, he was more a John Wayne. And to a young boy, the sunsets he rode into and the showdowns he had won were less impressive. Let's face it, to a kid seeing is believing. Ironically, this man merely represented one more era of baseball that played its role in creating the color and flare of today's unsurpassed double-knit millionaires.

Why then would a "nobody," especially one like me that has trouble spelling and a hundred-dollar car, become so motivated as to spend six years trying to defend and extend upon the theory of a living legend? It's simple. The man made sense. Not only did his theory aid me and a good thousand of my students in becoming better hitters, but also as a Physical Education major at Bridgewater State College I saw that Ted's theory repeatedly stood in line with the laws of anatomy and kinesiology. Hey, the bottom line is results, and Ted's theory won my respect and support because it *worked.* Considering the misrepresentation of Ted's theory, the logic it is based upon and where hitting is today, it's been six years well spent.

The following pages have been written to analyze, defend, and extend upon the Ted

The Globe and Mail, Toronto

UPI/Bettmann News Photos

Above weak hitting Blue Jay Danny Ainge drag bunts, while to the right, recognized as one of the best guards in the N.B.A., he plays a more popular role in the Celtic's dynasty. Due to the fact that Danny's obvious talents were stripped away in the skill of hitting, I feel his career becomes an ideal case study reflecting the important relation between one's ability and how it is perceived through the quality of their execution.

Williams' theory of hitting. With this book I am hoping not only to spark the comeback of decent hitting, but also gain the support of the men who lived the times and concepts I will speak of. As we go on, I am going to prove that when reaching potential is the goal, Ted's approach to hitting is not only the easiest, but also the basic approach for all good hitters, *regardless of their size and ability*. I challenge anyone to prove me wrong.

A Pitching Increase or a Hitting Decline?

At first I thought it would be easy. I figured by showing you a few graphs you too would immediately see the need for serious hitting renovation. Then I sadly realized that the majority of concerned baseball souls accept today's lack of hitting as the normal result of a *pitching increase* which breaks down to mean that everything I'm about to say is *for not* if you believe that on the average the hitters of today possess and execute a technique of hitting that is comparable or superior to that of the hitting in the past. Is it a pitching increase or a hitting decline?

I'll agree that on the average pitchers throw the ball a bit faster; man is getting bigger, stronger, and quicker. Would anyone disagree with a little more zip? I also think the defense covers more ground for the same basic reasons. Certainly deepened fences have helped the pitcher, and relief pitching has been his best friend. The use of relief pitching is undoubtedly a more effective defense against hitting. The skill of pitching has gotten better due to coaching's extended use of it.

But are these changes enough to place pitching head and shoulders above hitting? I say *no*. Hasn't hitting had its share of advantages to combat these factors? What about the lowering of the mound, the livening of the ball, astro turf, and the D.H.? Hasn't the hitter gotten stronger and quicker too, therefore allowing him to catch up to that faster pitch, reach those deepened fences, and get down the line? Physically speaking, I don't believe that it has become any harder for a hitter to hit a pitcher. I don't believe pitchers have gotten better. Now, I'm not saying that pitching hasn't dominated statistically; we both know that it has. What I'm saying is that it should not have, because pitchers and hitters are men, and man's basic physical abilities increase as a race. Pitcher's don't have a physical advantage. Their edge has formulated from the decrease of their rival skill. Pitching looks better because hitting has gotten worse.

Obviously, the next question is in reference to how this came about, and I'll explain that. But first think about this. Whenever I hear someone start defending a pitching increase or hitting decline, they always start talking about *statistics*. And why? Because statistics are easy for everyone to understand and talk about. But I don't believe this argument is based on statistics at all. Think about it. Statistics are only the results of different approaches or techniques. Stats are in the *past tense*. I don't want to argue over what has happened. I want to explain and convince you as to "how" and "why" this endless statistical argument has come about. I want to speak of and compare "technique."

When I say hitting has gotten worse, I mean that it is not *executed as efficiently* as it used to be in comparison to pitching. Ironically, convincing the hitting world of this fact is very difficult because there are no *technical statistics!* That is, we have no basis on which we can compare the hitting or pitching techniques and results of 1940 to today. Baseball has chosen to record too much of the *what* and not enough of the *how* and *why*. Consequently, hitting technique has found its way back to Square One.

How did this all come about? After great deliberation, I place the blame of hitting's decline on the changes within the skill's learning environment. In my experience as both a learner and teacher, I have found any successful learning environment to contain the following educational components: 1) enthusiasm on the learner's behalf to learn; 2) reliable information, along with someone qualified to transmit it; 3) "experimentation time," that is, a special time of practice and/or study where the learner tries to understand the worth of what he's been taught; and 4) a setting clear of unnecessary pressure and distraction. Due to the presence and quality of its educational components, my claim is that on the average, the learning environments of yesterday were far superior and therefore responsible for the success of the hitters that grew from them. While it is impossible to pick one year that marks the beginning of this gradual learning change; if we compare the average learning environment of 1940 to today, I'm sure you'll see the iron in my words.

In 1940, baseball as a form of entertainment and boyish recreation was unmatched. Baseball was truly the national pastime, and therefore the enthusiasm to become a hitter was at its peak. There were 43 minor leagues! More than 244 cities and towns supported teams. Kids and adults took more pride in playing and understanding the game because baseball was the Number One interest. Kids taped balls and nailed broken bats, while fans sincerely lived and died with *baseball's* teams and players.

Today the enthusiasm to learn is minimal. Baseball has entertainment competition ranging from several levels of different sports to MTV. Baseball is no longer the national pastime. Today there are only 17 minor leagues (*due to the invention of television, from 1948 to 1963 the existence of the minor league baseball player decreased by 70 percent*). Kids and adults don't take as much of an interest as they used to. Most have an interest in several pastimes. Kids don't tape balls or nail bats, and fans don't live and die with baseball's teams and players. Their interests and energies are distributed by choice over a wider span.

Reliable information and its transmission was also at a high in 1940 because you had great pro models. A kid going to see a major league game back then was getting his money's worth. Resultingly, the tips that these players passed on through magazines, newspapers, or over the radio were of high quality, and they were utilized effectively by inspired young hitters, coaches, or parents.

The overall experience level was also a great aid in transmitting decent information. Back then it was not that difficult for a learner to find and draw helpful information from someone that had actually hit or at least watched good hitting for a substantial period of time.

Technically speaking, today there are very few good professional role models; and as a result, we no longer have that reliable passing of good information. Today, accelerated by

merely the flick of a television set, we have a dwindling number of inspired learners carrying around subordinate *mental pictures.* (The mental picture is a physical education term regarding the stored information obtained consciously or subconsciously by watching a desired task. Many physical education authorities consider the mental picture to be the strongest influence in the learning of any skill.) The quality of the information that is passed through books, magazines, and television is horrendous, and the overall experience level is much lower. In all honesty, I've had trouble finding sensible hitting conversation at prestigious baseball camps — camps flooded with college and high school coaches.

Possibly 1940's greatest learning plus was the tendency to experiment and be creative. In the days of radio you had to imagine what was happening in a game and then figure out why. I think that kind of questioning and answering can be learning at its best. Also, the decade that follows a depression tends to grow kids that know *necessity as the mother of invention.* These boys would create a number of different sandlot games for any number of players or amounts of available equipment.

Today you can forget about experimentation and creative learning because kids aren't as self-entertaining; and they don't have to be. In our days, mothers and fathers pay networks and video games handsomely to entertain the minds of their children. As a result, many kids have become watchers as opposed to doers — copiers rather than creators.

I'm also convinced that organized youth baseball (1946) has put its squash on experimentation. Youth baseball provides too much instruction that takes away from the learner's natural instinct to sample different potential solutions. Certainly, structured youth play has retired a good portion of those sandlot games; and later I'll even show you how one of its ill-calculated dimensions also limits the learning of this skill.

Distractions were also at a minimum in 1940. Again, you didn't have kids being pulled by that elaborate selection of pastimes. There wasn't the pressure that there is today either, because kids played with friends — you know, the neighborhood gang. Organized youth baseball has brought the critical eye of adults and strangers into a kid's play. Hey, it's one thing when your pal next door says you rot, but it's another when it's his father or the kid across town.

The controversy over correct technique is an enormous pressure today. Everybody and their uncle thinks they know just how it's done, and the learner doesn't know who or what to trust. The flooded market of so-called *coaching aids* or *learning tools* designed and sold by people who, by all rights, should be wearing clown-suits is a whole world of hassle in itself.

My conclusion is that the good learning environments of yesterday regressed as a result of the changes within society. Society was growing towards *variety*, not only in sport, but also in recreation and entertainment. With this dramatic cut in baseball interest (not necessarily in numbers, mind you, but surely in depth), it wasn't long before the learning components I spoke of began to distort or deteriorate. It's really all very understandable. When you combine a loss of interest with the learning needs of the hardest single act in sports, it isn't long before you have a lack of knowledge and execution as well. It is a hitting decline.

A Change at The Top

Where is hitting today? After the cut of the minor league system starting in 1949, professional baseball became *thoroughbred baseball*. With teams signing fewer players, again a cut up to 70 percent, the tendency became to sign only those with *exceptional ability*. Professional play decided to rely on god-given talents; like foot speed, quickness, and strength. Out of line with Roger Hornsby's belief, pro baseball began to invest in hitters that "were born" and not made. The money once spent to harvest good execution was now used to find and sign raw talent. Ability had eliminated a good portion of the teaching phase.

Unfortunately, when these exceptional athletes came up to the big time, their abilities could *not* keep up with the hitting pace set by the superior execution of the past. Though, on the average, they were *physically* above the hitters before them, their lack of technique, along with the stability and growth of pitch-

ing, put them at a level below. Obviously, this lack of approach was more than apparent to the older hitters. These players, many times finishing their careers in the minors, did put forth a concerned effort to help, but the thoroughbreds wouldn't listen. Being the cream of the crop and potentially superior to the older hitters, their apprehension and ego created a *stick-to-your-guns* attitude. They decided to hang with the techniques that had brought them into professional baseball. Unfortunately and unknowingly, they turned their backs on good advice.

Now, this wasn't always the case; some young players did recognize their lack of technical quality and wanted to learn. However, the cutback of the minor leagues had taken away *their* experimentation time and added a hundred pounds of pressure. *(When a major league team has only four teams below it as opposed to "20," the name of the game is up or out.)* The days of learning and seasoning in pro baseball had gone. The focus had become immediate production rather than catered potential — a trade of overall talent for the quality of technique. In time, the hitters with the better techniques retired, and major league baseball slowly but surely became plagued with exceptional athletes possessing make-shift approaches. Who pays the price?

Well, not only does the professional never reach his potential, but as a result the hitters on all the levels below don't either. Let's not forget; pro baseball is at the *top* of the baseball totem pole! It is copied and respected as the finest of execution by all the leagues below it. With this decline of technique, suddenly major league players everywhere began passing on bits and pieces of conflicting advice. For example, one player may believe in the *downswing*, while another found success with a *level swing*. The result is a teaching and learning fiasco where the awe of pro baseball towers over logic.

Ironically, the *average youth*, the kid who *must rely* on good technique for his success has in the past and continues today to model an array of hitting tips that merely reflect the survival or trimmed success of a particular *exceptional athlete* in the major leagues. These talented but deceptive greats have and continue today to pass on advice that is not only *restraining* for the extremely talented, but *inconceivable* for the average. Regardless of why, professional baseball has shirked its responsibility to set precedent.

I think the fan is taking it on the chin, too, because he's seeing a lessened quality of baseball action. I mean, there can't be as many plays at third or at home. There are too many ground balls, strikeouts, and damn double-plays. If the ball was hit with good technique today, it would be hit much harder and more often than ever before. The game would be more interesting and exciting at all levels.

Strike Outs

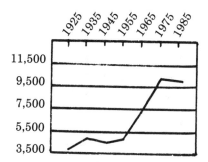

Double Plays

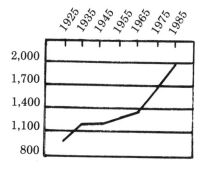

American and National League totals aver-aged per year and then over 10 year spans.

I'll tell you something else; I think our lack of hitting knowledge is also the main cause for kids to quit baseball and focus seriously on another interest. Hey, when you fail in hitting, you're all alone up there; and it only stands to reason that if a kid is striking out at the lower levels of baseball (little league, pony league), he may very well find his way to a soccer field. While it's true that he may not become a star soccer player, I feel on the average he *will* experience a greater amount of success and enjoyment, simply because the soccer people won't have a skill they can't teach.

Possibly the most intriguing part of hitting's mess is how it stays camouflaged. Because hitting is a skill of many timings taking place in an instant, good execution, in a sense, has always been hidden behind a wall of speed. Many of hitting's movements are very difficult for even a trained eye to follow, with some of them moving faster than the eye can detect. I know you're screaming that "slow motion" and freeze frame video had us behind this wall of speed years ago, and I'll agree that those aids can help us see what we haven't in the past. But those wonders came long after the cat was out of the bag. Slow motion replays don't help anyone when TV announcers are complimenting incorrect technique. Slow motion many times just gives a kid a better look at what *not* to do.

Add the lack of hitting knowledge today with the awe of professional baseball, and maybe you can understand why a guy like me has his share of problems trying to convince people that hitting is out to lunch. For some reason, most coaches, players, and fans tend to look at me funny when I start my case by claiming that the guy on TV making a million dollars a year could be much better. I can't blame them — again, they trust what they see! If a guy is strong, fast, and making big bucks, he's got to be good. Right? Think about it. It's just like when someone asks why they don't hit 'em like they used to. It's not the hitter's fault — his timing, grip, arms, wrists, hips, or preparation; it's that guy that comes out of the bullpen. "You're right, dad; he stopped 'em again tonight..."

The Mental Work Of Successful Hitting

Former Kansas City Royals hitting coach Charlie Lau (center right) is shown in dugout with Royals' Manager Whitey Herzog (left).

What About the Lau Theory?

Before we go any further, I'm sure you have heard the name Charlie Lau. Lau, a former batting instructor with several pro organizations, has also written a book. It's called *The Art of Hitting .300*. I would think the highlight of Lau's popularity was when George Brett (a former student) neared the .400 mark in 1980 with a .390 batting average. In the last few years I would have to say Lau has influenced more hitters than any other one person in the hitting world. However, I do not believe he has been a good influence. Frankly, I don't care for Lau's work because I feel he has prompted an approach to hitting that is mechanically unsound. Also, due to George Brett's demonstrative modeling in Lau's book, I have mixed feelings toward Brett as a professional. George

Brett does not hit the way Lau's book suggests. Ironically, Brett hits more like he walked right out of Williams' book. What could have possibly caused Brett to display the skill differently than he does in a ballgame? Unfortunately, due to both Brett's and Lau's position on the baseball totem pole, *The Art of Hitting .300* has been able to influence the hitting world to support unsound and detrimental principles that have begun and will continue to disrupt and restrain the skill of hitting.

Certainly, I don't blame Lau, because his work took place in the *worst* of environments. Hey, coaches are hired to be fired; and just because of that fact, nobody is going to tell me that many don't go along with things they don't believe in or understand to stay in good with the big time. Being a big league batting instructor is a tough job to lose; if people like you, you're going to be much better off. Now,

10

I'm not saying he didn't get more production from some players; I'm sure he did. I just feel that his work was *governed* by his environment. You *can't* teach a guy to hit when he makes eight times your salary. And most people just won't speak up as much when there's so much to lose. It's too much of a gamble. I feel as though Lau was not in a suitable environment to do any high level experimenting or teaching.

Lau certainly made many points that I totally agree with, and I feel his ability to teach those points had brought reasonable amounts of success to his students. However, the good points that Lau made were first presented to at least some degree twelve years ago in *The Science of Hitting*. In my opinion, Charlie Lau has really not said anything *new* that I consider helpful. I'll elaborate on the Lau Theory weaknesses as they become relative.

Know How it All Fits

In teaching the skill, I have found the best results to come from detailed explanations coupled with the individual hitter's natural progression. That is to say, it's best for the student to clearly understand what he's doing and why he's doing it before he moves on to something new. While it's true that you can work faster by simply fixing a hitter's weakness or weaknesses, I don't view that sort of repair work as quality instruction. Although the hitter may be an all-star while you're helping him, he's sure to fade when you leave. Then, without guidance, he will lack the knowledge to get back on the track. He will be back to Square One *alone*.

Now, you may think I'm making this sound more dramatic than it really is; honestly, I'm not. When potential is the goal, knowledge is a must. I'm talking about having the ability to make the right *corrections* and *adjustments* — the ability to *self-coach*. Hey, if you're playing a double-header in the middle of August, the sun beating down at 85 degrees, and the first time up you feel late on every pitch, you'd best be able to figure out why. A double-header could cost you *ten* poor at-bats

— ten poor at-bats! A hitter that can make the proper adjustments may only end up with *one* poor at-bat. Maybe he can adjust during that first at-bat, and end up with ten good ones. The hitter that can't make the proper corrections and adjustments is far below his par. This hitter will spend too much time pondering over the answers to elementary equations, not to mention the valuable at-bats he'll waste modeling flashpan advice. Knowing right from wrong and why is the place to be. This is why a good batting instructor is invaluable. If a guy knows his stuff, he can detect and correct problems before they actually become problems. By playing guardian angel to the entire lineup, a good batting instructor can eliminate pounds of pressure and instill tons of confidence.

Unfortunately, good batting instructors are rare items, and therefore the knowledge has got to come from the hitter. With this in mind, I have written this book much like I teach — in *progressive detail*. I want you to know *how* and to know *why*. I want you to be able to coach yourself, or even better to teach another.

A Few Definitions

I have found definitions to be one of the hitting world's largest problems. The hitting world tends to underdefine, and this only adds to its confusion. To avoid any further misunderstandings, I feel it's important for you to see how I define certain hitting terms. I'm sure this theory will be much easier to understand and apply if the hitter and/or coach consciously note the components and stipulations on which it is based.

Hitting: Hitting is the *seasonal* battle of *mind and body* against the oppposing team's pitchers and defense in a *game situation*.

Technique — Approach: A good hitting technique or approach is a logical batting philosophy *combined* with sensible and effective mechanics used by the hitter in such a way that will not only allow him to hit the ball as *hard* and as *often* as possible, but will also allow the hitter to reach as many *total bases* by hit, walk, or error.

Talents: Talents in hitting are the tools of a hitter's capabilities. A hitter's talents are both *mental* and *physical* and dictate his potential. They include attitude, intelligence, observation power, patience, vision, coordination, quickness, foot speed, strength, and stature.

(Please note the term "Style" will be addressed in detail a bit later.)

Attitude is No. 1

When I think of the perfect hitting attitude, I think of a movie. In a scene from "Rocky II," Rocky's trainer, Mickey, is telling Rocky (a left-handed fighter) that he must learn to fight right-handed to protect a bad eye and confuse his opponent. When his trainer finishes, Rocky says, "Hey, Mick, I can't learn to fight right-handed no more," and Mickey says, "What's 'can't'? There ain't no 'can't.' "

As a batter, unless you're just beginning to hit for the first time, chances are you will have to make some changes or adjustments. They may be mental or they may be mechanical, but they *won't be easy*. You may want to say, "I can't." *Don't do it!* If you want to be a hitter, there ain't no "can't"!

What is "can't"? "Can't" is a copping-out word that implies laziness or fear of failure. "Can't" is easy; "can't" is convenient. "Can't" is a quitting word; and as a hitter, it's a word that has no room in your vocabulary. 'Can" is a much better word. "Can" implies self-confidence and determination. When we speak of the "can" and "can't" viewpoints of anything, we are basically speaking about the most common ingredient in any success recipe — *attitude*. Except for health or eyesight, the most prevailing item necessary for successful hitting is attitude. If you're going to have any shot at all at becoming a good hitter, you must maintain a progressive and inquisitive attitude. You have to want to get good and want to know how. Remember, we're talking about becoming superior at a very complex skill. You have to love it. While coaching the Washington Senators, Williams was known for in-spiring desire, provoking conversation, and stimulating thought about hitting. As a player, they used to say that Williams lived for his next time at bat. He wanted to hit; he wanted to be good. He wished it on every falling star. Good hitters must *want* to be good hitters, because as you're probably starting to see, the odds are strongly against a hitter's progression. I think I'm coming in loud and clear when I say, *"if you don't want it, you won't get it."*

In hitting, more than in other skills, the want and dedication has to be amplified in the player; because unlike other sports, a hitter isn't going to get the proper instruction, practice, or support he needs to progress correctly. For a hitter it is an absolute must to withhold a positive attitude reflecting dedication and determination. The hitter must be like a *shark* — his survival thriving on both his insatiable curiosity and relentless motivation toward progress. Only this attitude will enable a hitter to combat today's difficult task of learning proper technique and then utilizing it to his potential.

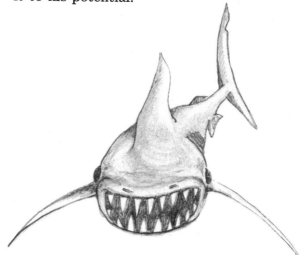

The hitter must be like a shark — his survival thriving on both his insatiable curiosity and relentless motivation.

Think about it. If you want to become good at something very hard you best have a crackerjack attitude to tackle it. Certainly, you wouldn't fish for tuna with five-pound test line, nor would you hunt for elephant with a BB gun. Likewise, it's important that you don't try to become a hitter with a pin-the-tail-on-the-donkey attitude.

Get a Good Pitch

After the birth of a good hitting attitude, your next goal is to understand the mental work behind a hitter's success. In *The Science of Hitting*, Williams said that hitting a baseball was 50 percent from the neck up. He claimed first and foremost that a smart hitter must get *"a good pitch to hit."* But is it a high pitch? A low pitch? Inside? Outside? Or right down the pipe? Is it a curve ball? A fastball? A slider? What is a good pitch to hit?

Off the top of my head, I'd define it as a pitch that you have not only *anticipated*, but also one that comes within an area that is *appealing in relation to the count.* While this definition conveys the basic idea, I'm afraid that unless we break it down, most will never really come to grips with its value.

Anticipation

Let's take a look at the word *anticipate*. To anticipate in hitting is to *guess* or to *look* for a particular pitch *before* it has been thrown. Make no mistakes here; with *less than two strikes,* I'm talking about an all-out decision to prepare for one type of pitch and only that pitch. If another one comes, I'm *not* going to swing. I will *take* that pitch even if it's a strike. I know, I hear it all the time. You're wondering, "Why guess? Why not just hit whatever is thrown?" You figure if the pitcher has three pitches, two-thirds of the time you'll be off; and at that rate, taking strikes left and right.

Well, first off, a hitter guesses for timing's sake, and I'll talk about timing in more detail; but for now, please note that hitters guess because it gives them a much greater chance of hitting the different pitches they *must* face. The hitter facing a pitch that he has not anticipated is at a grave disadvantage. The speed of the unexpected pitch will *jog* the hitter's timing. If the count is 2-and-0 and you guess fastball and a fat curve comes right down the pipe, a good hitter will *take* that pitch because it is not what he is looking for, and therefore, *not* what hs is *prepared* to hit. The hitter's body is in no position to hit that pitch with *authority* (will elaborate). *With less than two strikes, a good pitch to hit must be a pitch you* *have anticipated.*

If the pitcher has the ability to throw different speed pitches, doesn't it seem logical that the hitter should try to *prepare* or *adjust* for the probable speed? You bet it does. In simple terms, that's what timing is. Unfortunately, the hitter doesn't know what's coming; and therefore, in order for the hitter to prepare himself *mechanically,* he must first consciously decide what pitch is probable. He must guess.

As far as accurate guessing goes, I would like you to think about another Ted Williams' statement. He said, "The beautiful thing about baseball is that the *hardest* pitches to *hit* are the *hardest* pitches to *throw.*" To me, that remark is brilliant because it isolates the true battle between the pitcher and hitter and alleviates some of the doubt over a hitter's ability to think along with the pitcher. Hey, when the count is 2-and-0, the pitch most likely will be a fastball; and when the count is 0-and-2, the pitch will probably be a breaking ball. And why? Because fastballs are easier to throw and breaking balls are harder to hit. There's no big secret, it's simple logic. For the most part, when the pitcher is behind in the count, like 2-and-0, he isn't going to risk throwing a pitch that is more difficult to control. Why risk letting the count go to 3-and-0 and then be pressured to throw the strike? More times than not the pitcher will come to you. Remember, *"a walk is as good as a hit,"* and because of this, you can count on certain pitches at certain times. A .300 hitter *fails seven out of ten times* — seven out of ten times! Unless the hitter is a true longball threat in a tight situation, the pitcher would be foolish not to throw the fastball 2-and-0. As you will hopefully experience, guessing along with the pitcher is *not* a difficult task.

Naturally, as you go up in baseball, the pitcher tries to throw the pitches that are *not* probable: and sure, sometimes the pitcher will be throwing his breaking ball just as consistently as his fastball — maybe even more so. Please don't misunderstand me. I'm *not* saying when you have a 2-and-0 count, you *always* look for the fastball; or when it's 0-and-1, you *must* look for the curve. I just want you to understand what the *bulk* of your anticipation should be based on.

When Williams spoke of guessing years ago, he said that guessing came from a framework — a framework created by *observing* the pitcher and storing up information for future use. It's not really *guessing* at all. The term "guessing" implies a decision based on luck or chance. I'm talking about a *calculation* — a *calculation* based on the review of data. Ted referred to this as *doing your homework*. He felt the hitter's past and present observations would enable him to think properly at the plate — enable him to guess correctly. Let's face it; all pitchers are different; and if you're going to get to know their tendencies, you've got to take notice — *you've got to watch*. I know that's a hard thing for many guys, but that's the way it is. They're not going to throw the good one all the time; and therefore, *observation is a key*. It gives us our game plan for each at bat.

AP/Wide World Photos

Boston Red Sox pitcher Roger Clemens releases a seventh inning pitch against the Baltimore Orioles at Boston's Fenway Park Saturday on the way to his thirteenth consecutive victory while undefeated in 1986.

As far as I'm concerned, there are three main *observation times* of equal importance: 1) *any time the pitcher warms up*; 2) *when you're at the plate*; and 3) *when the pitcher is pitching to someone else*. During these times the hitter will be asking and answering certain questions about the pitcher. For example: are his pitches down or up? What is his best pitch? When does he throw it? How did he pitch to you last time? What did he get you out on? Does he pitch different with runners on base? Answering questions like these will allow the hitter to think along with the pitcher. For example, let's say you watch the pitcher warm up and he only shows two pitches, a fastball and a curve (which is many times the case in high school baseball); he faces two hitters before you and throws three curves in the dirt; you step up to the plate and the first pitch is a fastball outside; you say to yourself, "Well, the curve hasn't been over, so I'm guessing fastball." The pitcher throws it and you hit a home run. Now, the next time up you say to yourself, "No way will he throw me the fastball," due to the homer, and you guess curve ball, first pitch. This time he throws the curve for a strike. Now you say, "Well, he's up on the count by throwing the curve and I hit the fastball last time, I'm going to guess curve again. Here it comes, *bang*, line out to the shortstop; but you're proud of a good at bat due to logical thinking.

On the other hand, if he had struck you out your first time up with, say, a called fastball and two swinging curves, your second time up you'd be crazy to look for the fastball because he's convinced the curve is the pitch for you.

Obviously, these are basic examples, and the tendency is for many people to claim that, "Ya, when there are only two pitches, guessing can be easy. However, when you get to the college or pro level, where you find three and four pitches, you can't guess." I think these people are selling themselves or their players short. When you learn and feel the benefits of a good swing, observation, and guessing (again, something that's been lost today), you won't be so quick to throw all this credit toward the pitcher. His ability and pitch selection won't be so impressive because your decisions and movements will make you quicker, stronger, and more consistent.

Also, when you're a good hitter, it gets much

harder for the pitcher to mix them up, that is, to risk throwing something other than his *best*. Sure, he might have four pitches, but when you're a good hitter he starts to worry about throwing his lesser pitches. When a hitter establishes himself with the pitching in his league it makes it easier to guess because the pitching tends to challenge him with their very best rather than an arsenal of different pitches.

Location

What is an acceptable location in relation to the count? It is no more than playing the percentages; that is, *striving for a ball that is deserving of our swing with regard to the situation.* I feel getting good location is best executed by setting up three hitting areas. The first area is called *the rip area.* It is the area in which the hitter feels he can hit his best, and it should encompass about a quarter of the hitter's strike zone. The rip area will be used when the hitter is up on the count. The hitter will now refrain from swinging even at an anticipated pitch that is not in his rip area, and that's important. Photo 1a shows my personal rip area. However, keep in mind that yours may be totally different, as seen with a different hitter in Photo 2a.

The second area will merely be an extention of the rip area and will not only include the rip area but will include two-thirds of your strike zone. This second area, which I call the *even area,* will be used on all counts with one strike. (Photo 3a outlines both my *rip* and *even areas,* while Photo 4a outlines the other hitter.) Again, the hitter would not swing at even an anticipated pitch that was outside the even area.

2a shows a different style hitter who's mechanics prefer a different area.

3a includes the "even area", this area, an extension of the rip area, is used on counts of 1 strike.

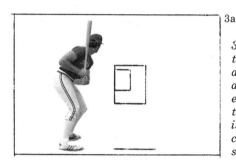

4a shows the other hitter's rip and even areas.

The third area is your strike zone and also includes what Williams calls the *gray area;* that being the area around the strike zone where strikes are sometimes called balls and balls are sometimes called strikes. This area is used whenever the hitter has two strikes on him. (Photos 5a and 6a outline all three of the areas, including the gray area.)

1a displays the "rip area", used when up on the count, it is the area the hitter hits best.

5a relays both these areas inside the strike zone and what Ted called the "gray area".

6a

6a gives us the other hitter's rip and even areas inside his strike zone along with his gray area.

I think you can understand the importance of using these areas correctly. According to Ted, "a good hitter can hit a pitch in a good spot three times better than a great hitter can hit a ball in a questionable spot." If I go up to the plate and ground out on a 2-and-0 pitch on the outside corner at my knees (a place where I don't hit as well as others), I'm a fool! I have literally helped the pitcher to get me out. Williams will say that pitchers are lucky to face hitters so dumb, and he's right.

Nothing is easy and, unfortunately, there is still one more very important factor. Williams called it *knowing yourself*. In Ted's book there is also a great hitting statement by Lefty O'Doul. O'Doul, another great hitter, said that most hitting faults come from a lack of knowledge, uncertainty, and fear; and that boils down to *knowing yourself*. Knowing yourself means knowing *your* strengths and weaknesses. Do you hit the curve ball well? Is the high fastball a problem? Do you have trouble picking up the slider? Truthfully knowing the answers to these questions and questions like them will dictate whether you know yourself or not, and this becomes important when defining a good pitch to hit. The reason I say this is because your definition of a good pitch to hit can *change daily* when you compare the pitcher's strengths and weaknesses to your own. For example, if the curve ball is your major weakness and you're facing a good curve ball pitcher, you'll probably be better off waiting for the fastball. A step further, *you may look for that fastball in the even area when you're up on the count. You may decide to concede some location on the fastball to avoid your weakness with the curve.* On the other hand, if you're facing a pitcher whom you can completely handle (a pitcher who does not have a pitch you can't hit) you're going to wait for the anticipated pitch in the area you want it.

Again, each time you play, your definition of a good pitch to hit will be based on the pitcher's strengths and weaknesses in relation to yours and, like a poker hand, *each pitcher will have to be played a bit differently.*

How to See

After understanding the requirements of a good pitch to hit we must now learn the finer points of literally *reading* the pitch to decipher both *what* it is and *where* it is. We must learn *how to see.* After the pitch is released, the hitter will begin to absorb information in a split second. Fortunately, when this information is processed correctly, it will enable the hitter to identify both the type of pitch and its location. Because most pitches travel at different speeds, *speed* becomes the first clue when trying to identify the *type* of pitch. To identify a pitch by its speed, the hitter must *grow accustomed to the feelings he can receive from the oncoming pitch's speed in relation to the speed of the pitch he had anticipated.* The feeling he'll receive will answer the question, "Are you on time?" which is much like asking "Have you guessed correctly?" or "Are you getting what you anticipated?" I call this reading or answering period *timing feel.* Because a solid understanding of timing feel requires more mechanical discussion, let's put it on hold until we discuss the term *timing* in more detail. However, please keep in mind that a pitch's speed is the *first* clue in its identification.

The next clue is the look of the ball — the spin and the color. After the speed checks out, the rotation and color can make all the difference in the world. Take the slow curve and straight change, for example. Because they may be traveling at the same speed the hitter watching a straight change, waiting for it to break, may end up being late. However, if the hitter was able to identify this pitch as a straight change by its color and rotation, he probably would not have waited as long. Certainly the slider has a unique spin as opposed to the fastball — a crucial clue in its identification. The sinker would be another example;

16

many sinkers appear much whiter in color than fastballs due to the grip and release point they are thrown from.

There is one other type of clue that a hitter may also receive, and that's a *tip-off*. Williams spoke of how he could sometimes immediately identify a curve by the way certain pitchers really had to snap it off to get it going. These motion clues, or tip-offs, are inpurities in the pitcher's delivery that give a pitch away, and naturally they can be a great advantage. However, I don't believe they happen often enough to make them a major concern. For our purposes, I'll say that if a pitcher gives something away, fine; however, don't spend time looking for or trying to *invent* a tip-off that is not there. As we've discussed, there are better things to be concerned with.

To determine *location*, I feel that it is good practice for every hitter to think about the ball as if it's traveling in a tunnel. This tunnel starts out small over the pitcher's shoulder and increases almost to the size of the hitter's strike zone. Diagrams 1a and 1b show what I mean from two different angles. To master the use of good location a hitter must begin to learn where a pitch will end up (in his or out of his strike zone) by noticing *a relation between the ball's location when it's passing through an early point in the tunnel, and then its location at the plate*. I call this *tunneling*. The advantage of this lies in the fact that a tunneling hitter can see a pitch at *one point in time* and understand where it will be at *another*. The hitter is able to detect the pitch's location long before it gets there, therefore improving his pitch selection — enabling him to use his areas strategically. Diagram 2a shows a hitter using a reference point in the tunnel.

1b

Here, what I call, "tunneling" is seen from two different angles. The advantage of this lies in the fact that a tunneling hitter can see a pitch at an early point in time and understand where it will end up. The hitter is able to detect the pitch's location before it actually gets there, therefore improving his pitch selection.

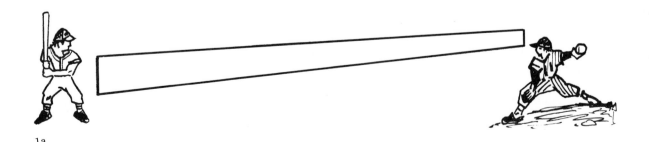

1a

2a

Here a "tunneling hitter" understands the location of a pitch long before it reaches the strike zone.

These reference points also have areas much like your strike zone, they have *their own private rip areas and even areas.* If the count is 2-and-0 and you're looking for a rip area fastball, you would be looking at the rip area in your fastball reference box, which connects the pitch to your rip area at the plate. This can be seen in Diagram 3a.

Now, the curve ball has more of an arc and also has more downward and lateral movement; and because of this, the right-handed curve ball reference box will be higher and to the left of the fastball box. Diagram 4a shows both the fastball and curve ball boxes and also how pitches coming through the off-centered curve ball box will end up in the strike zone. (For left-handers the box, of course, would be basically the same height but to the right.)

Also, the height placement of these boxes depends on the speed of the pitch. Though the boxes would be equal in size, a 90-mile per hour fastball would have its box lower than a 75-mile per hour fastball; and this is important to note. Diagram 5a displays this idea.

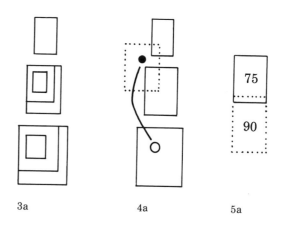

3a   4a   5a

Diagram 3a shows that the reference points, much like the strike zone, have their own connecting "rip" and "even" areas. 4a displays the different placement of a breaking balls reference point, while 5a conveys their height difference dictated by the pitch's speed. One should note that 5a's boxes are placed somewhere between mid and ¾ flight.

After seeing a pitch one time in a game situation, a good hitter should be able to set up a reference box for that pitch. I feel that boxes can and should be created for all pitches that follow a regular pattern; for example, fastballs, curves, or sliders. However, a reference box will be useless against a pitch that tends to move on an irregular pattern. The best example being the knuckle ball.

In closing this section it would be foolish not to include and support another apropos Williams' statement — "Don't swing at anything you haven't seen," which means if possible, *don't swing at a pitch you have no information on, no timing feel, no reference box, no rotation or color.* Most times if a hitter swings at a ball he hasn't seen before he won't hit it hard. By watching a pitch just once you'll gain an edge on the pitcher's motion; you'll feel the pitch's speed; see its break (if it has one); you'll be able to set up its tunnel box and see both its color and rotation. You will have gained valuable information, making the pitch an easier pitch to hit. This is why Ted called the first at bat of a game *"the key up."* The first at bat is geared toward gaining information by *making the pitcher pitch.* The first at bat is the hardest — it's almost a time of sacrifice. But if you get a look at everything that first time up the other times will be much more fun.

Now, I'm not saying you go up there and take strikes foolishly, but if you can see a pitch before you have to swing at it, that's the goal. For example, let's say you're up for the first time and first pitch you see a fastball outside for ball one. So now you guess fastball rip area for the next pitch — whoosh, here it comes. If you take that pitch you should be shot because you've seen the fastball, so if it is in the location you hoped, go ahead and swing. But if that second pitch was a curve, I wouldn't swing in a million years. I'd rather gain the information from seeing it and wait for the next pitch.

The Moves Of
The Hitter

if you don't have one you wont hit write

The Moves of The Hitter

Like life itself, in hitting time is the most valuable thing you can have. Everything you do will be done to give you more time; whether we're talking about stance, the weight of the bat, position in the batter's box, length of stride, or the shifting of the weight, the bottom line is *time*. The more time you have, the better. Williams calls this the heart of hitting. He will say, *"The more time you have, the less chance you have of being fooled."* Remember, if that ball is traveling at 90 miles per hour, it will get there in about four-tenths of a second; you'd better have time or it's going by you.

every thing comes down to this

I have learned that time at the plate is developed by solidifying certain mechanics in the swing. These mechanics work together to not only give you more time, but also the power you need to hit the ball hard and with consistency. Important at this point is to note that in hitting, the movements are *intertwined* so that they not only rely on, but affect one another. Therefore, all of the following me-

chanics will be *equally* important when trying to develop a good swing. Because of this, I suggest you carefully examine and attempt all of the mechanics I present, noticing not just their individual worth, but their dependence on one another.

Before we talk about the hitter's movements, let's take a quick look at stance. While I agree that everybody has their own personal stance, I also believe there are several important ingredients necessary to make any stance a good stance. I like to see a hitter with his knees and waist slightly bent; his feet should be about shoulder width apart, with the front foot slightly open and the back foot straight across. The body weight is *evenly distributed*, not forward on the front foot or back on the back foot. The stance is *balanced*, with the weight falling through the center of the body, and both arms are *bent at each elbow joint.* — *not back elbow sticking strait up*

I feel the hands should start just below the top of your strike zone and relatively close to the body, about three to eight inches away. The body is comfortable; the midsection untwisted, with the head straight up and the eyes *level*. The hitter's feet are *flat* on the ground, making his base stable. The hitter's body is *relaxed* with his mind on one specific speed pitch in one general area.

Okay, bubble gum and sunflower seeds at arm's length? Pride and ego all warmed up? Let's talk about the movements of the hitter — his mechanics.

The Pre-swing
(the cocking motion and stretch position)

The first phase of movement is the phase that *prepares* the hitter to hit the *probable pitch* with both consistency and authority. I call this movement phase the *pre-swing*. Now, please note that the pre-swing is nothing new. Williams identified it years ago as the most important move of the hitter, only he referred to it as the *cocking of the hips*. Naturally, we are talking about the same movement. However, I am breaking it down into two separate stages. I have done this because I feel the phase that Ted identified has some other important movements that must be recognized. *Regardless of what you call it — the cocking of the hips or the pre-swing — let me caution you now that if this phase of the swing is not understood and executed properly, the hitter will surely run into problems.* needs a good instructor

Williams referred to hitting as a pendulum — a movement back, followed by a movement forward — "a move and counter move." The first movements of the pre-swing, which I call *the cocking motion*, represent the hitter's backward flow of that pendulum. The cocking motion begins *before* the stride and when the pitcher starts to break his hands in his wind-up, although this can vary. It is executed by bending the back knee *straight down* and the front knee *in and down at the same time.* These body movements should be *smooth* and *comfortable*, like a pitcher's motion. *The bending of the two knees will cause the body not only to shift its weight more onto the back leg, but also to twist in towards the plate.* These movements can be seen in Photos 7a and 7b.

8a   8b

8a and 8b show how the heel lifts as the front foot rolls onto the outside of its big toe.

Also the hitter should note that in the cocking motion, his entire body will *lean into the plate just slightly.* This is done by the hitter coming onto the *ball* of his back foot from a *flat-footed stance.*

Looking at the top of the hitter, his eyes will not leave sight of the pitcher, with the head as still as possible. Also, as the body flows back, the hitter should think about his front shoulder *turning in and down*, much like his front knee. This is important. If the front shoulder was to rise up too much in the cocking motion, the hitter would then have too much weight *back*, which will lead to a slower swing.

An interesting factor to point out is that in the cocking motion, the eyes and angle of the front foot control the *distance* of the hitter's backward rotation. If the front foot was to point back to the catcher or if the head turned back so that the eyes could not see the pitcher clearly and completely, the hitter would have gone back *too far*, placing himself in a difficult position to execute his next movements properly. swing is blown

7a   7b

7a and 7b display "the cocking motion." It is achieved by bending the back knee straight down and the front knee in and down at the same time.

not picked up off the ground

If I had to pick one movement of a hitter's mechanics that I considered to be the most important, it would be the second move of the pre-swing, *the stretch position.* I feel this way because *the stretch position is not only responsible for placing the body in a position of potential speed and power, but it is also where the hitter starts his counter move forward — it's where he gets his body going.* Concluding the cocking motion and when the pitcher's arm

During the cocking motion the *heel* of the front foot will lift, causing the foot to *roll up* onto the outside of its big toe. While this is happening, however, the *angle* that the front foot was on in the *stance* (slightly open) will not change. This can be seen in Photos 8a and 8b.

not to
for

is over his throwing shoulder, the hitter will smoothly twist into the stretch position by *striding and opening his front foot* while trying to *rotate his front shoulder back toward the catcher.*

While it would be feasible to consider the stretch position the result of two individual movements, I prefer to view it as one. Although the hitter is making one movement by rotating his hips forward with his stride and another separate movement by making an additional attempt (besides that of the cocking motion) to rotate the upper body back, these movements are occurring again *in unison* and therefore I consider them to be components of one large parting movement. *Remember, the hitter is rotating his upper body and lower body in different directions at the same time.*

9a   9b

Photos 9a and 9b show these opposite lower and upper body movements to the stretch position. Notice after the cocking motion how the front *toe* is *opening out*, while the front *heel* travels only a *short* distance. Also notice how the upper body turns back at the same time, while the arms remain relatively still (I will elaborate). Why are these movements so important?

By rotating the upper body and lower body in different directions, we are *stretching the muscles that indirectly connect these segments*; and as a result, tying or connecting them directly together. That is to say, that we are preparing or positioning the body in such a way that when the lower body begins to rotate forward, it will *immediately* pull the upper body behind it.

Before we observe the results of the stretch position in an actual swing sequence, let us first see the same concept displayed with these simple illustrations (Diagram 6a.)

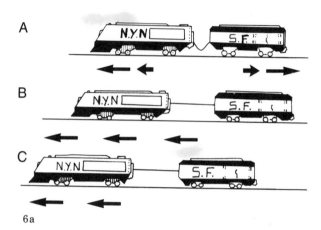

6a

Example (A) presents two toy train pieces: an engine and a boxcar. As you can see, these pieces are connected by a rubber band that lies *with slack* in between them. Naturally, the engine is much heavier than the boxcar and, unlike the boxcar, possesses the ability to pull things. Now, if the engine was started and driven slowly to the left, while at the *exact same time* the boxcar was shoved once, making it move slowly to the right, the rubber band would begin to stretch, and as the rubber band continued to stretch toward its potential, both the engine and boxcar would slow down. However, because the boxcar is lighter and does not have a continual source of drive, it eventually would stop and be pulled in the opposite direction by the engine, as indicated by Examples (B) and (C).

Whether it's a hitter's upper body and lower body, or two pieces of a toy train, when we move them apart we are preparing the muscle, or elastic, between them to *tow* the lighter piece, the upper body, or the boxcar, directly *without any slack*. Therefore, we now tow the object without *delay*. The effect of the stretch position on an actual swing becomes vivid when the following swing sequences are compared.

The first photo sequence, Sequence 10a-c, relays a swing launched from the stretch position. Notice after the cocking motion how the front foot and front shoulder have traveled *apart*, insuring a good stretch position and deleting any possible slack between the two.

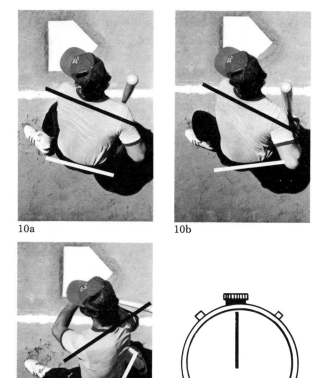

10a   10b

10c

From the stretch position, there is no lag time between the lower and upper body.

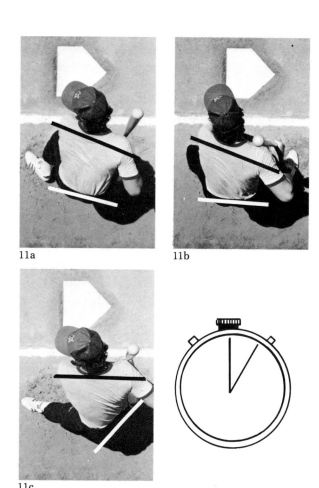

11a   11b

11c

Without the stretch position, time is lost before the upper body responds.

Also notice how, after the decision to swing is made, the lower body and upper body respond at the *same time*. Because the upper body and lower body were set apart in the stretch position, they now move as *one unit*, no different than the two train pieces. When the lower body rotates, the upper body *must* follow.

On the contrary, Sequence 11a-c demonstrates a swing that has been launched from a poor pre-swing — a pre-swing that had neglected to form the stretch position. Notice after the cocking motion how only the front foot and hips begin to open, while the front shoulder remains stationary, therefore overlooking the parting movement necessary for deleting the slack. Notice how the hips are free to open after a decision to swing without any coupling to the upper body and therefore *the bat*. Also, pay particular notice to the *time* that has passed on the clock before the re-

Don't Forget the Importance of the Stretch Position!!

sponse of the upper body.

The conclusion here will be an old story by the end of this book; it's *the loss of time and power due to incorrect movement or preparation*. If we take two hitters, all things being equal except the utilization of the stretch position, the hitter who executes it properly will be much quicker. The *no slack* connection of the upper body and lower body will force his upper body and bat response to be *immediate*, therefore enabling him to view the ball *long-*

24

er before he must *commit his swing*. This hitter has more time and therefore will see the ball longer and receive clearer information, resulting in better pitch selection and a cut-down of times when he would have been fooled. On the other hand, the hitter that does not prepare properly will swing with an unnecessary delay — a lag time between body segments. This hitter sees every pitch *seemingly faster* than it is and must commit himself earlier to make up for his slower swing. This hitter does not see the ball as long before his swing and is forced to *condense* his information. Naturally, he must make rushed decisions, causing him to be fooled more often by both the type of pitch and overall location. It's interesting to note how a neglect of good physical execution can cause mental breakdowns.

Neglect of the stretch position also results in another loss — and that's *power*. Now, when I say power, please don't misunderstand me; I don't necessarily mean long balls. I mean power in relation to your style — in relation to your personal potential. Looking at the swing with power in mind, the lower body and upper body represent the swing's two greatest sources of *momentum*; and without proper execution of the stretch position, these two momentums will be used separately and consequently inadequately. Much like gaining time, for power potential the swing must start with the lower body directly pulling the upper body behind it. The baseball swing is a kinetic chain — a full body gyration.

For a practical example of this concept, let's say you and your friend have been hired to knock down a wall, and to do the job you rent two identical bulldozers. After you fire them up you each take a shot, one by one, at ramming the wall, but the wall won't fall. After coffee, your friend says, "Let's drive them into the wall at the same time." Boom! Down it comes, a job well done...I'm sure you can see what I'm getting at. Every hitter has two bulldozers — two major weight areas that contribute to creating the hitter's swing momentum. These areas are the upper and lower bodies. And the only way a hitter can tap their *combined momentum potential* is by driving them together from the stretch position. *The baseball "swing" is a full body movement that funnels its momentum down to the point of contact.* Naturally, we want all the mo-

mentum available.

Due to the importance of the stretch position, it's important to check its quality periodically. This can be done by having the hitter freeze after he lands his stride, and then while holding this position the hitter searches for the feeling of *slight tension* in certain areas. If a hitter does not feel any tension in these areas, something may be out of sync and he best review. In Photos 12a and 12b, we see the stretch position with a labeling of these common tension areas. Please note, however, that these tensions will go unnoticed in an actual swing due to the short space of time in which the muscles are stretched.

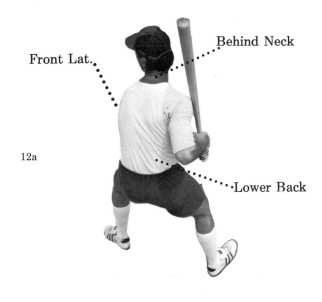

12a

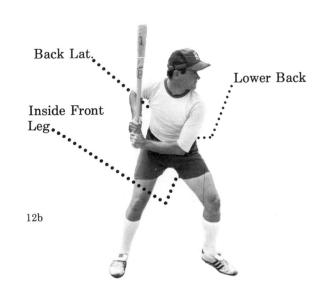

12b

Landing and Hip Rotation

Pushing on, like Ted I've found that *hip rotation is the true root of batting speed and power.* However, to acquire good hip rotation the hitter must learn to use both his *legs* and *weight* properly. Again, proper execution demands good preliminary positioning, and here we are setting the stage for good rotation by *landing the front leg correctly after the stride.*

During the flight period of the stride, the front knee and foot will remain in the *same position* that they assumed in the cocking motion. This means that the toe will be pointing down with the knee turned in and down. Due to the outward rotation of the hips during the stretch position, the entire stride leg will be opening up to the pitcher in a *fixed position.* The only front leg movement is an outward rotation of the leg from the *front hip.* Photos 13a and 13b show the stride from the cocking motion. Notice how it then lands in that same position, with the toe touching down first and the knee still *bent.*

14a · 14b

14a and 14b display how the stride brings the hitter to a balanced position — a position where his weight is evenly distributed.

Notice how the upper body eventually becomes situated in between the front and back feet, with the front shoulder slightly down. Also notice in Photo 15a how the foot lands on the inside of the big toe. (Actually, the pressure is at the base of the toe, not at the top.) Assuming that the pitch is timed correctly, a hitter landing properly will be at the peak of his physical preparation. What happens next?

13a · 13b

13a and 13b convey how the front foot "opens" in a fixed position and lands that way with the toe touching down first.

Another very important element of landing is *balance.* When the hitter lands that stride foot correctly, *he should feel his body weight follow to a point of balance — that is where his weight, like in his stance, again becomes evenly distributed between the front and back feet.* This can be seen in Photos 14a and 14b.

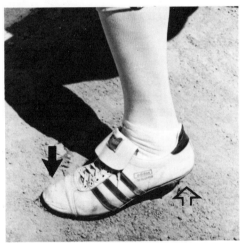

15a

Photo 15a lets us see how the front foot lands on the inside of the big toe. The pressure is felt at the "base" of that toe.

26

If the hitter chooses to let the ball go by, the pendulum movement will stop when the hitter lands. However, if he decides to swing, the pendulum will continue harmoniously into the rotation of his hips. As you can see in Photo Sequence 16a-d, when the hitter decides to swing from a balanced position, that is, a position where his weight is evenly distributed from leg to leg, *the bent front leg begins to extend — begins to straighten out*, therefore pushing the front hip back and around the corner towards the catcher. Meanwhile, at the exact same time the back leg, which has also *remained bent* from the cocking motion pivots on the ball of its foot. Due to its bent position, this in turn thrusts the back hip forward and around its corner (Photo Sequence 17a-d).

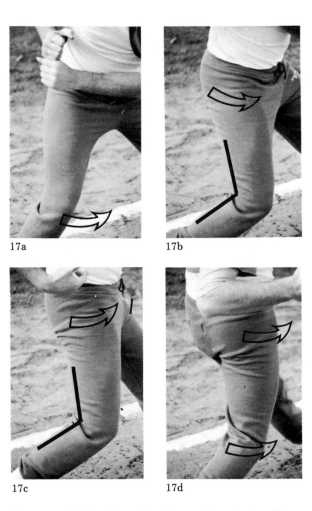

17a 17b

17c 17d

Sequence 17a-d tells us that the rotation of only a "bent back leg" will thrust the back hip forward.

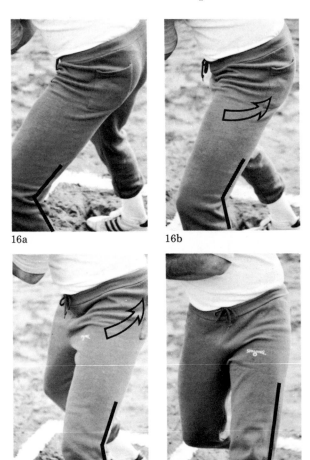

16a 16b

16c 16d

Photo sequence 16a-d shows how a straightening front leg should push the front hip back. This can only start from a leg that has landed in a bent position.

What good technique demands is two separate forces at opposite ends of the lever, *pushing in unison* in opposite directions. The result is a *pinwheel type movement* — a rotation of the hips by *both* legs. Diagram 7a shows the concept.

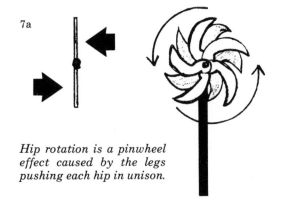

7a

Hip rotation is a pinwheel effect caused by the legs pushing each hip in unison.

Important to note is that if the front leg had not landed correctly after the stride — if it had reached out, as in Photo 18a, extending the knee *prematurely*, the front hip would be left with no *power source* to push it. Now the hitter would have to rely solely on the rotation of the bent back leg, which is just not enough. Hitters that reach out their stride leg by extending their stride knee prematurely are left with less momentum when it comes time to hit because they have eliminated a power source. It's much like asking someone to hop without first bending their knee. This is another reason why that front knee must *turn in during the cocking motion*. The hitter is bending it more to be used later in the swing.

Here in 18a, if the hitter's front knee reached out prematurely, the hitter will have no "power source" in which to push his front hip.

18a

Just as important and relatively similar is the preparation and use of the back leg. If the knee of the back leg is not bent in at least the stance, the back hip will not thrust forward because its power source is a pivoting *bent* back leg. If that leg is not bent the hitter will depend solely on the front leg for rotation, and again, that's not enough. *Good hip rotation depends on the proper use of the legs that support it.*

Considering the task involved, along with how the hips and legs are connected, to start hip rotation the weight must be *evenly distributed* on both legs. If the weight remains too far *back* or comes too far *forward*, there will be too much weight on the *back or front leg*, slowing down and restricting its movement.

As you may already suspect, *balance* is one of my arguments against the Charlie Lau theory. In *The Art of Hitting .300*, Lau states

and lists in his "Absolutes of Good Hitting", that you hit off your *front foot*. Naturally, I disagree. The swing starts off *both feet* because this is the position in which the hitter can begin the strongest and quickest *rotation*. Ironically, as the body rotates, the axis tilts *back* just slightly. Supporting the path of a slight upswing, the hitter must take more of his weight on the *back leg*. This can be seen in Photos 19a and 19b. The ideal baseball swing starts off *both* legs and then favors the *back* leg.

19a

19b

Photos 19a and 19b show the ideal baseball swing starting from "both legs" and then favoring the "back"

UPI/Bettmann News Photos

Think about it. If you were to continue coming forward to hit off your front leg (which used to be called lunging), you would undoubtedly run into problems (Photo 20a). This is demonstrated from cover to cover in Lau's book by George Brett, who, by the way, in my opinion has a very well-balanced swing in real life. First of all, you would immediately become slower with the bat and cut down your reaction time because now your average contact point will be much closer to the pitcher's release point. Comparing Photos 21a and 21b, we find a difference of about three feet — three feet! Have you ever hit a ball at the label? I know you've hit a few on the fat part. The way I see it, the label is an out and the fat part is success. How far are those two points away from each other on the bat? Not very far. So why give the pitcher a three foot advantage when just a little can slaughter you?

You won't get good hip rotation off the front foot; you can't, because when your weight is over your front leg your cleat will grip tight

20a

Here, photos 21a and 21b compare the different contact points of the Lau and Williams approach on the same pitch. Photo 21b marks both points to convey the loss of time in the Lau theory. The upper left photo shows the starting point.

21a 21b

older, to avoid 20 minute conversations during games, I learned to say, "Yah, good sinker."

There's another factor, too. When you come forward you're coming forward with your head and eyes also, and you've now created *two* timing variables. I mean, now the ball is coming at you while you're coming at the ball. If I threw 500 tennis balls at you while you were standing still and then 500 more when you were jogging toward me, in which situation would you be more successful? Standing still, of course, so why try and time two things instead of one? It makes no sense.

The low ball is definitely harder to hit off your front leg because your eyes are further away and you have to reach more, which is another can of worms entirely. Viewing Photos 22a and 22b you can see how much closer my eyes are to the ball when swinging with balance. Does Lau list a little extra hand-eye coordination as an absolute of good hitting? He should because you'll need it if your eyes are farther away or moving up.

22a 22b

Front foot hitting not only causes the eyes to rise, but also, (22a, 22b) to be further away from the contact point.

in the dirt and that front leg is just not going to open. Sure, I've seen those hitters who seem to possess the ability to spin their leg around while their foot is cemented in the dirt, but that's unnatural and certainly not very healthy. To me it's more like something Moe would do to torture Larry. I'll tell you right now the average guy can't move like that — not to the extent that is necessary. And if you base part of your success on something that's anatomically unnatural, I don't think you're off to a very good start. Do you?

Certainly hitting off the front foot makes seeing the ball much more difficult because, as you come onto the front leg, your eyes have got to come *up*. I've known front foot hitters to come back to the bench claiming the pitcher has a great sinker. So I'd get up and, sure enough, no sinker. Hey, it's simple — the eyes go up, the ball appears to go down. As I got

Hey, I'm not saying a ball can't be hit hard by coming on to the front leg, it's really just a golf swing; and there is plenty of momentum. But in hitting, unlike in golf, *it is impractical because there is a time factor.* A golf ball is not moving at you. You don't have to catch it at a specific time out of the air, you just have to hit it. In golf your momentum *can* be created by *lunging forward*, but in hitting it must be generated from a *circular pattern*. What people forget when they start talking about

30

swinging and power is the actual task involved. Swinging for maximum power and hitting are two different worlds! I'm not writing a book about how to hit a baseball as hard as you can, and neither was Williams. We have written books about hitting balls as *hard and as often* as you can. Williams' technique observes and caters to both *power and timing combined.* Lau's front foot swing is inferior in view of the task. The Lau *lunging* swing requires more natural ability to be successful: you need a greater percentage of physical and mental quickness, better eyesight, more flexibility, and hand-eye coordination.

Why do people use it? It's easier. The Lau swing is an *easier* swing to learn. Unfortunately, as its followers climb the baseball ladder, they may very well wish they worked harder and followed logic, because while the Lau

swing is easy to learn, it's much harder to hit with. Sure, the Williams stroke requires some work, but so does everything else that's worthwhile. Certainly it's not *that* hard. The *swing* is no more difficult to learn than shooting a basketball. It's merely good instruction and practice. Photo Sequences 23a-d and 24a-d demonstrate bad and good technique.

24a 24b

24c 24d

Sequence 24a-d runs through a swing starting from a balanced position and then favoring the back foot.

23a 23b

23c 23d

Photos 23a-d display front foot hitting, actually in accordance with the Lau theory my front foot has "opened" too much.

The Movements of The Arms

I don't believe there is anything more aggravating than to watch a hitter execute perfectly and then blow it all completely out the window with the arms, wrists, or hands. Unfortunately, it happens all the time and at all levels. And as you will see, even if a hitter is moving good before and during the swing, improper use of the arms, wrists, or hands will bury him. Yes, it's true that the preswing will *prepare* the hitter for ultimate bat speed and power; and yes, good hip rotation will then create it. But a hitter has got to realize that only the proper use of his arms, wrists, and hands can then *apply* what he's created. Remember, these body parts control *the bat!*

When speaking about arms, I find it best to slowly trace their movements through the entire swing. Beginning with the stance (Photo 25a), we again see both arms bent, with my front arm *slightly tense* and my back arm — my power arm — relaxed. The next photo (25b) displays the cocking motion. Here again we see how the arms do not move on their own, but merely rotate back with the upper body *as one unit* and in the same position. As we go on to the stretch position (Photo 25c), the arms pull back *slightly*; however, the movement is in the *front shoulder joint*, while the elbow joint of the front arm does *not* change its angle, and that's important.

Up to this point I have found the arm movements to be fairly easy to both learn and teach. However, after the hitter decides to swing, we find the movements to be much more difficult. Holding off on the reasons behind this difficulty, at this point it's important to introduce another phase of the swing that I have identified specifically to help the teaching of proper arm movement. I call it the *dip phase*. The dip phase will start immediately after the landing of the front foot and a decision to swing. The dip phase is actually the *beginning* of the swing — the beginning of *hip rotation*.

Now, in the dip phase we see not only the rotation of the back foot with a bent back knee (Photo 26a), but we also see how the *back half* of the body is *dipping* or *lowering* (Photo 26b), leading the hips, arms, and bat into the slight upswing. The bottom arm is still bent, but now traveling *up and out of the way*, while the top arm (still bent) has *tucked close to the body* (Photo 26c). The arms really have *not* moved much from the basic position they maintained in the stance. If you think about it, it's the movement of the upper body that has changed their position by dipping and rotating forward. Hence, the old saying "Don't drop the back shoulder," is an untruth.

25a

Stance

25b

Cocking Motion

25c

Stretch

26a

26b

In the "dip phase" we see not only the rotation of the back foot with a bent back knee (26a), but also the back half of the body dipping or lowering (26b).

26c shows how in the dip phase the front arm remains bent and now travels up and out of the way while the bottom arm tucks close to the body.

26c

As I mentioned before, the *front* shoulder should turn in and down as the hitter prepares and lands, but this is *before* his decision to swing. Once the hitter *starts swinging*, the *back* shoulder must drop in and down and then come up with the swing as the body rotates forward. Now, with the hips having led the way, both bent arms will extend, the bottom arm *pulling* as the top arm *pushes*. These movements again are in *unison*. This can be seen in Photos 27a and 27b.

Here with a piece of cardboard I've displayed these movements again. Notice how the elbows crush the cardboard.

27a

27b

While we're on the subject, the dip phase is also helpful in distinguishing important timing landmarks — its identification in teaching lets a hitter know where his hips are in relation to his bat and shows him the value of moving specific body parts at specific times. For example, Photo 28a shows not only how in a good swing the back foot, back knee, and bat will begin rotation together, but also how the hips truly lead the entire swing.

With the hips having led the way, now both arms will extend in unison. The bottom arm "pulling" while the top "pushes" (photos 27a and 27b). Note photo 27b is a bit "after contact.

28a

Why do I want *tension* in the front arm? The answer lies in the fact that when a hitter starts his hip rotation, the circular momentum that's created places an overwhelming *jerk* on the front arm, causing a natural tendency for it to then *drift back — straighten out.*

It is here where the movement difficulty I spoke of begins because, in short, the front arm must *combat* this strain and prevent itself from straightening out *too early.* I call this *anchoring the front arm*, and it's done best by preparing the arm for this *sudden strain* with a slight bit of tension right in the stance. With this tension, the bent front arm will now first *pull* the bat and power arm around with the rotation of the upper body guarding and preserving the position of the bat and arms in relation to the upper body. This allows both arms to remain bent while they await a double arm extension into the potential contact area. Both arm movements can be seen in Photo Sequences 29a-d and 30a-d.

29d

30a

29a

30b

29b

30c

29c

30d

Why all the caution? If the front arm pre-extends, whether it be in the stance, cocking motion, stretch position, or beginning of the swing, (the latter being the most common) the hitter will run into problems by changing the length of the lever in which he is swinging. With the front arm extended, the hitter now swings a lever that ranges in length from the end of the bat to his front shoulder; the shoulder being the pivot point. Photos 31a and 31b display the common problem of drifting the front arm at the beginning of the swing. Notice how the front arm has extended and now how it begins to drag the power, or top arm, out and away from the body as well. The drawbacks are endless.

31a

31b

Photos 31a and 31b show the common tendency of a hitter pre-extending his front arm at the beginning of his swing.

First off, the hitter is now using a *longer, heavier lever*, that being, of course, the arm and bat as opposed to just the bat. Naturally, the hitter is slower and therefore loses time by having to commit himself (decide to swing) earlier. Also, the hitter is moving that lever (at least in the front arm) with a different group of muscles — the shoulder muscles — and it's much more difficult. How fast can you move an outstretched arm and bat from Point A to Point B as seen in Photos 32a and 32b? Not very fast — it's much too heavy! Proper execution relies upon *the upper arm muscles*, not the shoulders. We want to use the muscles that control and support the extension of the *elbow joint.*

32a

32a and 32b display the lenghthened level caused by pre-extendation. this long heavy hitting tool ends up causing the hitter a world of grief.

32b

The problems continue. If the arms do extend early, they will cause the hands and bat to travel in a *circular path*, and while a hitter's body certainly *rotates*, the bat and arms merely ride with it until it comes time to *apply* the momentum your body has created. At that time the arms fire the bat *straight to the ball*. This can be seen best in Photo Sequence 32c-e, where the dark line represents a high inside pitch. In Photo Sequence 33a-c we see improper arm movement caused by pre-extention. Notice how the pre-extended arms bring the hands and bat into contact in a circular path, where Photo Sequence 32c-e displays the arms pushing into contact in basically a straight line. Naturally, the shortest distance between two points is a straight line and therefore the curved path of Photo Sequence 33a-c has cost the hitter valuable time. The pre-extended hitter is geometrically slower (Diagram 8a).

While I've got pre-extension with its back to the wall, let's look at its effect on the *potential contact area* (the area in which it is *possible* for the bat to hit the ball). When a bat approaches the path of the ball with a

32c

32d

33a

33b

32e

The good hitter starts his rotation with both arms bent, then, like the tail end of a whip, fires them "straight" into the contact area.

33c

The pre-extended hitter's bat travels in a "circular" path. This longer heavier hitting tool now appraoches the contact area from the side.

8a Geometric Comparison of Arm Paths

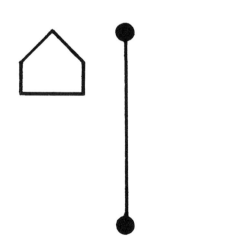

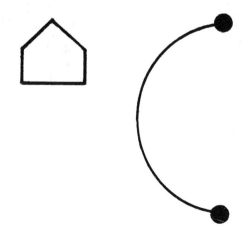

8a shows a geometric comparison of correct and incorrect arm movement. In this simple diagram we can observe the lengthened path of the pre-extended hitter's hands and bat. It will take this hitter a longer period of time to reach contact.

circular attack, it approaches more from the *side*, cutting down the possibility of contact by literally cutting down the amount of *time* the bat is actually *in* the potential contact area. In Photo Sequence 34a-d, the dark line again represents the path of an inside high pitch. Notice how long the fat part of the bat remains outside of the potential contact area due to pre-extended arms where, in Photo Sequence 35a-d, correct arm movement keeps the bat in the potential contact zone much longer. The conclusion is that the pre-extended swing not only cuts contact percentage, but also requires better timing on the hitter's part.

35a

35b

34a

34b

35c

35d

Here, good arm approach keeps the better parts of the bat in the contact area throughout the entire swing.

34c

34d

The pre-extended hitter will not have the preferred parts of his bat in the contact area anywhere near as long as good technique. His contact potential is resultingly reduced.

It's not over yet! The pre-extended swing also causes the ball to be hit much further to the left for a right-handed batter or to the right for a left-hander which, by the way, often is well foul from an even stance (I'll elaborate). This can be seen in Photos 36a and 36b.

Though I'll talk about this in more detail later, where the ball is hit on the field is an element of your *style* and extremely important. This problem of hitting balls more to the left or right stems from the angle in which the hitting surface of the bat comes into the contact area. A step further, in Photos 36a and 36b, we see not only the *approaching angle* of the bat but also the *available batting surface* provided at contact by correct and incorrect technique. This concept may be easier to understand (Photos 37a and 37b) where I have displayed the same basic arm approach with

37a

37b

36a

36a shows the approaching angle of the pre-extended hitter's bat. From an even stance this pitch is way foul. The lines on the bat display the available hitting surface that this angle creates.

36b

36b displays the approaching angle of a bat launched from good arm execution. Please note, the angle in which the ball will be hit, along with the increased contact area.

With a tennis racket, 37a and 37b compare the available batting surfaces of the two approaches.

a tennis racket. As you can see, correct arm execution will also provide a greater batting surface along with balls hit in their proper direction.

Another hassle is that pre-extended arms create a *weaker hitting lever*. Remember, in the pre-extended swing, the hitting lever is from the *shoulder* to the *end* of the bat, and this lever has two major weaknesses; the elbow joint and the wrists. Due to the length of the lever, both the elbow joint and wrists will *give* quite a bit at contact, costing the hitter a valuable loss of power. While it is true that the wrists and elbow joints also give with proper arm movement, the arms are *behind* the contact — *behind the lever* as opposed to beside it, and therefore the give is much less. These weaknesses can be seen in Diagram 9a.

Also, with proper arm movement, the attacking lever is only the length of the bat and therefore composed of *a consistent substance being wood or aluminum* as opposed to wood or aluminum plus bones and flesh. The pre-extended hitter must be much stronger to both swing and support this faulty lever.

I'll tell you another thing: balls hit toward the end or handle of a bat supported correctly are hit much harder, therefore the hitter with proper technique has more room for error. He'll end up with more *blood hits*. Levers compared in Diagram 10a.

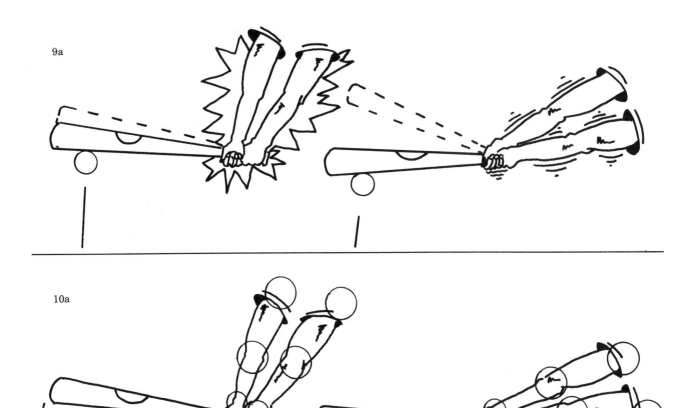

9a

10a

Certainly, the pre-extended swing's *lever weight*, makes the pre-extended lever more difficult to control and therefore *less consistent* when trying to hit such a small target. From the angle of Photo 37c, we can picture the pre-extended hitter's tendency toward vertical fluctuations, while the same hitter swinging correctly swings a lighter and more *controlable lever due to technique* (Photo 37d).

37c

37d

My final blow at pre-extension relates to my comment on keeping the arms and hands close

to the body in the stance. Although not as noticeable, the heavier lever is also harder for the entire body to swing. The hips and upper body will not rotate as *quickly* if the arms drift away from the body at any time.

My conclusion is that the pre-extended hitter must be stronger, quicker, have better timing, and the ability to make rushed decisions. The hitter that finds success with pre-extension is miles from his potential.

I'm sure you can see why I'm so concerned with using the arms correctly, but I think my case becomes even more dramatic when one understands that, mechanically speaking, pre-extension is possibly hitting's most common and destructive problem. Very rarely do I observe good arm execution at any level, and it hurts to watch it needlessly wither away at good contact percentage, and therefore baseball action and interest. However, when a major league batting instructor demonstrates excessive pre-extension as proper technique (pages 122-130 of Lau's book), it's not hard to understand why.

Plate Coverage and Bat Selection

If you're on the ball you may be saying to yourself, "Sure, that was a great explanation of arm execution, but you can't reach the outside corner that way and, therefore, it's useless." Well, I don't think it's useless, it's perfect technique, but you would be *correct* about the outside corner. With good execution, 26-inch arms, while standing 13 inches away from the plate in an even stance, I need a 36-inch bat to deal with the outside corner. Now, I'm a fairly big guy, 6'2", 200 pounds, and what I'm getting at is that the smaller guys with the shorter arms are even less *capable* on the outside of the plate and therefore should use *longer bats*. Through the eyes of good mechanical execution, the bats most hitters are using today are much *shorter* than they should be, and it's putting a damper on the comeback of good hitting. Naturally, whenever I say *longer*, which many times means heavier as well, everybody starts screaming bloody murder. But when we make an example of Ted himself, standing 12 to 13 inches off the plate using a 35-inch bat with about 27-inch arms (armpit to palm), what I'm saying starts to sound very logical. In relation to Ted's arm length and the distance he stood from the plate, a 35-inch bat was necessary if he was going to use his arms correctly and still be able to cover the width of the strike zone. What I want you to realize is that if Ted had used a 33-inch bat he would have had to sacrifice one of two things; either bat speed and power, due to the need and use of pre-extension for plate coverage, or plate coverage on the outside corner due to the shorter bat. The point becomes clear — *the smaller armed hitter is getting railroaded and he doesn't even realize it. He's swinging a shorter, lighter bat with pre-extended arms, losing bat speed, power, and consistency when he could be faster, stronger, and more consistent by using a longer and heavier bat swung correctly.*

I know what you're thinking . . . the smaller guys with the smaller arms aren't strong enough to handle the longer, heavier bats.

You're *wrong*. The shorter armed hitter isn't *physically weak*. He's much stronger than he's given credit for, but he hasn't had the platform to prove it. He has been *forced* to pre-extend by circumstances beyond his control, and as a result he has become *mechanically weak*. Certainly, you can understand that how you use your body — its angles and their movements — will have a direct effect on your efficiency. Well, this is the problem with the shorter armed hitter. He is less than what he could be (slower and weaker) before and during contact. He is using his arms incorrectly and using the wrong bat.

When people wonder why some of these smaller stocky guys don't hit more home runs, many times they need not look any further than the bat in the hitter's hands and the way it's being brought into and supported at contact. Think about it. Do you think Ted Williams possessed any more of a natural ability to hit home runs than Pete Rose? No way! What makes a powerful hitter? It's *momentum* (a weight times a velocity). And when momentum is applied correctly, the more you generate — the harder the ball will be hit. Though Williams was taller than Rose, I don't believe Ted had the ability to generate as much momentum as Pete. Lau's book lists Rose at 192 pounds in 1979, which is very close to Ted's *mature* playing weight of 190 pounds. However, Pete has been a much faster runner than Ted, which breaks down to mean that Pete has had the leg ability to move his 192 pounds much faster than Ted's 190 pounds. I think you can see where I'm going. What dictates the speed of the swing? *Hip rotation.* And what controls hip rotation? Legs.

A step further, if we had them both in their prime, who would you bet on to *bench press* (an exercise that requires similar movements and the same muscles as good arm execution) the most amount of weight? Sorry, Ted. Rose has clearly possessed long ball ability. *Why* hasn't he been more productive in the power categories? It's plate coverage, bat selection and pre-extension! Rose's power, like so many other hitters, has been lost from the shoulders down. Mechanically speaking, Williams made up for and surpassed Rose's *natural* speed and *untapped* power by using the bat that would allow him to use his arms correctly, and therefore apply his momentum more

AP/Wide World Photos

AP/Wide World Photos

efficiently. Now, please don't get me wrong. This comparison is not to down Pete Rose. He is truly a *great*. But I feel the comparison relays the important fact that the shorter armed hitters have been, and continue to be, forced toward the wrong bat, pre-extension, and therefore, an inferior hitting approach. How and why has this happened?

Again, looking at the major leagues as a role model, I'm sure one reason has been the decrease of hitting's overall study and available instruction. The difficulty of anchoring the front arm correctly (one of the hardest mechanical achievements), coupled with a decrease of instruction and practice, slowly but surely lured the model hitters into the natural tendency of pre-extension. Once hitters were pre-extending, it then became logical to use a shorter, lighter bat because if you're pre-extending, a lighter bat will help you. Unfortunately, you know what happens next. Bat manufacturers start following the model trend, and they start making shorter, lighter bats, and before you know it we have a *vicious circle of regression*. Today, more than ever, pro hitters aren't apt to make a drastic change like

I'm suggesting. Would you go out on a limb with your 1.5 million? They'll keep the light, short bat trend alive, which is okay I guess. It's a free country. But if you're a *young hitter*, the pro hitter of the future, you suffer too. The young hitter can't get the bat he needs because the manufacturers won't make a personal model unless it's for a pro. So really, pro baseball's pre-extended, short-bat trend is restraining all of hitting, and you must see that. I'm lucky — I've got 26-inch arms, and I can still dig up good 36's. Ted was even more fortunate. However, if you've got shorter arms or stand further away from the plate than I do, you've got a problem. According to Hillerich & Bradsbery, they don't make a bat over 36 inches. In fact, their wood comes cut at 36 inches, which is sad because most of the hitters that play this game have *shorter* arms than I, and therefore they immediately have a bat availability problem.

You know, it's funny — the hitters of yesterday used longer, heavier bats. Why? Man was *smaller;* they had *shorter arms* and *weren't* as *strong*. Why would they ever want to reach for a larger bat? According to Hil-

Above, my next door neighbor, Ryan Jones (12) helps me present the unjustified relation between our bats, arms and the plate we hit off.

lerich & Bradsbery, there were many bat orders over 36 inches. And remember, this was when baseball was booming, highly competitive — truly the national pastime. Where is the logic? The way I see it, hitting was indeed much better; and on the average, these *smarter hitters* knew how to use their arms and understood not only that they needed a certain bat to execute to potential, but also that good mechanics could swing that bat efficiently.

Let's talk about the little league plate? Do you know that little league baseball uses the same plate as major league baseball? They *shouldn't*; neither should pony league baseball. In a 500 kid sample, I found kids from ages 10 to 12 to have 19½-inch arms; that's 6 inches shorter than mine. Also, on the average, they used a 29-inch bat; that's another 7 inches off their plate coverage. However, the width of the strike zone remains the same. The little league and pony league hitter has no choice but to reach — to pre-extend.

It's the same story every time: a young kid starts out at a lower level of baseball with poor instruction on a 17-inch plate, and he starts reaching. Before you know it, from a lack of results, he grabs a lighter, shorter bat and does better. Ironically, now the hitter thinks he's on the right track because he doesn't understand the effects of pre-extension. Sadly, he continues to pre-extend and faces the skill with the bat that pre-extension has *demanded*. As a result, very few hitters start out using the right bats and therefore never learn good mechanics. It's a rut, and it's not going to change until baseball makes some changes.

Little league baseball should shorten the plate's width, not only increasing the length of the bat in a sense, but also forcing the pitcher to sacrifice speed for accuracy. Let the good young pitcher begin trying to get hitters out by moving the ball and changing his speeds. This could take place easily at a *slower overall speed*. The pitcher dominates little league baseball, and it makes the game *boring*. The *outfield* is not even in the game; and as a result, very few boys want to play out there.

They look down on playing the outfield, and it's only because there's no action out there.

We *can't* forget fear. Most younger little leaguers (9-11) are scared to death at the plate. Today's strike zone allows a strong 12-year-old kid to reach back and let it loose. And if it's going 45 miles an hour at little league distance, that's like 60 miles an hour at major league distance. That's faster than Bill Lee, and too fast for little league learning.

I talk about the plate, but really, in youth baseball we must see a dual change — a lengthening of bats and a shortening of plate width. Certainly, you couldn't just extend the bats because then they would be too heavy or frail, nor could you just shorten the plate's width because the pitcher would have control problems. There's a ratio to be found here between length of bat, size of arm, and width of the plate. It really wouldn't be hard to find.

Sure, most will think I'm crazy for saying that a guy like Rose would be much better off with good arm execution, and a 35-ounce 37-inch bat (just a guess), but isn't it funny, the rules read that a bat can be up to *42 inches long*. Is that a foolish rule? I wonder how many plastic baseball authorities of *today* are smarter than the game's creator?

Assuming you can have any bat you want, how do you find the one that's best for you? When first selecting a bat I recommend, as Ted did, that you choose something that feels good in your hands — something you think you can handle. However, this can be confusing because real good bat selection can only occur after the hitter adopts a sound mechanical approach. How can you pick a bat before you experience your length need, speed, or strength with good mechanics? I know my bat changed drastically with the development of my swing. And just as I have seen when teaching, the tendency was toward something longer and heavier.

After you *can* swing, the ideal bat for you is a bat that will enable you to cover the outside and low pitch with good arm execution and still be quick up and in. The best way to find it is to stand at the plate the way you would in a game and go through your swing in slow motion with the outside and low strike in mind. When you reach the assumed contact point, you freeze and examine your mechanics (especially your arms). If they're good, you've

got your *length*; and now you simply test its *weight* against the high heat you'll face. There's an experimentation period here, and it's an important one. Take your time.

Going a bit further on the subject of bat length, if we were to picture all hitters standing in the exact same batter's box position, I feel the combination of bat and arm length from the outside corner of the plate into the front shoulder should add up to be about the same distance for all hitters. Listen, everybody's got to cover the same distance, whether it's with a longer bat or longer arm. This is seen in Diagram 11a. Unfortunately, today we have a relation that's more like the one seen in Diagram 11b. And it just doesn't add up.

11a

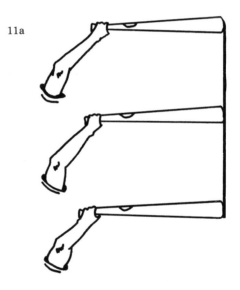

11b

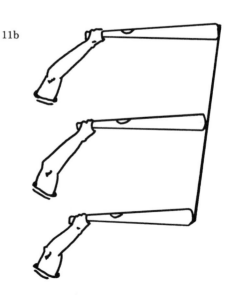

Above, my good friend Bill Adams helps me convey the proper positioning of the arms, hands and wrists at contact.

The Wrists and Hands

Moving down to the wrists, we find them extending with the arms; not only creating additional momentum, but also controlling the angle in which the bat head makes contact with the baseball. Photos 38a and 38b illustrate the bat head's movement caused by the wrists.

38b

38a

Also important is the position of the wrists behind this approaching bat, which Williams called *unbroken wrists*. The bat must be supported *correctly* at contact. And as you can see in Photo 39a, my wrists are *behind the bat — behind the collision.* Unfortunately, many times players will have their hands over the bat at contact, losing proper support and therefore complete application of force. This is what Ted called *rolling wrists.* It's a common problem and it will hit your batting average like a wrecking crew (Photos 40a and 40b). In these photos it's important to notice the position of both hands and how these positions could easily allow the bat to be pushed *backward*. Now the hands, the bat's key supporters, are in a weak position to support it in relation to the direction of the oncoming ball.

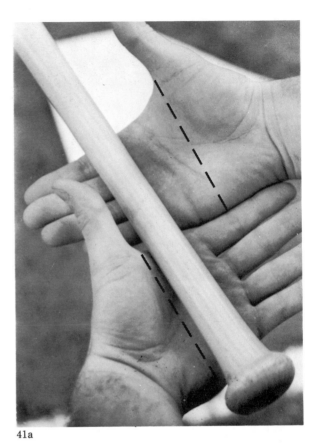

41a

Like Ted, I feel the bottom hand should hold the bat like a hammer while the top hand holds it more in the fingers.

39a

At contact, the wrists are positioned "behind" the bat, while the arms meet the plane of the pitch.

40a   40b

40a and 40b give us a good idea of what "not to do" with our wrists. Also, note that rolling wrists will cause the bat to hop toward the top of the ball.

The name of the game is to have the least amount of *give* at contact. If some of the momentum goes toward pushing the bat backward, the projection force will be decreased and the hitter will lose a great deal of power. *Hey, we want the bat to push the ball, not the ball pushing the bat.* In front of having strong wrists and forearms is the fact that the contact point must be *mechanically strong — mechanically sound* with unbroken wrists.

Learning how to make proper contact brings us to another subject of importance — *grip*. How you hold the bat in your stance will have a direct effect on how well your hands support it during contact. Like Williams, I feel the bottom hand holds the bat like you would a hammer, while the top hand holds it more toward the fingers. Photo 41a illustrates the bat's placement in each hand. The grip should also be *firm;* you don't hit a baseball with a *limp* grip; and no matter how many fingers are moving in a guy's stance, if he's good, when he starts to swing, he holds on *tight.* Now, Lau warns against what he called *white knuckles,* claiming that a tight grip can cause tension in the whole swing. Well, I believe a player can have tension problems in his swing, but I don't believe it stems from holding the bat too tight. Just because your grip is firm doesn't mean your upper arms must be tense. These body parts are controlled by two totally different muscle groups. Can you squeeze a rubber ball without flexing your biceps? Sure you can. If you know what you're doing and if you practice and learn to control your body, tension won't be a problem. I think people overdo the tension thing. Like statistics, tension is something everybody can talk about, so they do. I think, much like Lefty O'Doul, that tension comes from *fear, uncertainty, and a lack of confidence.* If you're tense, it should tell you that you've got some learning to do.

Lau also feels that your grip should be firm, but *relaxed* with a personal knuckle alignment. I don't agree. How can your grip be firm and relaxed? That's like trying to sleep standing up. To me, firm is firm and relaxed is relaxed. If I have to apply any pressure, I'm not relaxed. You can only have one or the other; and when you're trying to turn around an 80-mile-an-hour fast ball, it best be firm.

I don't like his theory on knuckle alignment either. I feel there is a *universal* knuckle alignment: counting from the fingertips, *the second knuckle on the index finger of the top hand lines up between the second and third knuckles on the bottom hand.* I believe this to be the best grip for covering all locations with good support at contact. I'll tell you, though, if I knew a guy was going to keep it at my knees all day, I might consider moving my second knuckles closer together because that's a better position for a low ball; and on the other hand, if a guy was up letter high all day, I may consider moving in the other direction; that is, top seconds toward bottom thirds. The problem is that the majority of the time you don't know whether they're going to keep it down or up, and therefore you're better off playing the percentages with the grip I suggested. This alignment is seen in Photo 42a.

Now, in your stance, this knuckle alignment usually feels a bit *uncomfortable*; don't let that bother you. Remember, you don't hit in your stance — *you hit out at contact*, and this grip is comfortable out there where it *counts*. If you settle for a comfortable grip in your stance, watch what can happen. Photos 42b and 42c show a common comfortable knuckle alignment and the problems it can lead to at contact. Notice how the wrists and therefore the arms are not really *behind* the bat at contact, leaving the bat less supported than it could be and therefore more vulnerable to *give*, whereas in Photo 42d we see a proper knuckle alignment leading to a position where the fore-

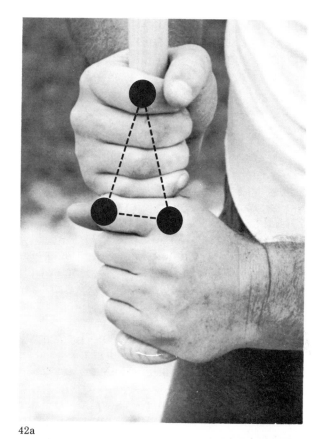

42a

42b

42c

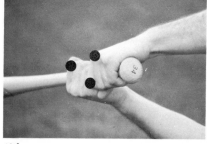

42d

The photos above show proper and improper knuckle alignments and the contact points they lead to.

arms are behind the bat, giving full support.

A hitter should note that after·a week of this knuckle alignment, much like riding a new bicycle, the discomfort or newness will disappear. *Don't associate comfortable with right.*

Now, I've heard people argue that a hitter should *squeeze on contact*, and while it's true that you would be just a little quicker doing it that way, I don't advocate it because I don't believe the contact point is easy to *predict*. If you're late squeezing, you may lose a hit due to frail support at contact, even though the swing was perfectly timed. Also, the tendency is to move your hands around the bat when you swing, that is to say the swing momentum changes your knuckle alignment. Another problem with it is that when you squeeze, the bat tends to move vertically. Hey, if it rises one-quarter of an inch, you could lose out.

The bottom arm wrist, much like the bottom arm, can also be thought about as a part of the swing that *guides*. The bottom wrist controls (from the pitcher's view) how the bat is positioned horizontally at contact. Naturally, to increase contact percentage we want the bat to be *level*. In a full swing — that is when the arms fully extend into the ball (we will talk about other strokes where they do not) — the bottom wrist will fluctuate the position of the bottom hand from *up on the low ball to down on the high ball*. These movements will keep the bat as *level as possible* throughout the different heights of the strike zone. Photos 43a, 43b, and 43c show the position of this wrist for a level bat at three different strike zone heights.

Now, you may claim that I'm contradicting myself on the high pitch because the bottom wrist is not totally behind the bat and therefore not supporting the bat as well as it could. Well, though *both* the arms, wrists, and hands support the contact point, the *top* arm, wrist and hand — the ones *closest* to the contact point — *supply most of the support to the collision*. The way I see it, the bottom hand's first job is to let the top hand do its job correctly.

That reminds me, one of the worst sayings I've ever heard in hitting is *top hand over*. This is used by people who believe that hitters roll their wrists at contact, and it's par for the course because if any hand was thought to be

Looking straight on, these photos compare the angle of the bat as it approaches the ball, To increase contact percentage, we want it to be as level as possible.

High

43a

Mid

43b

Low

43c

coming over slightly at contact, it would be the bottom hand on the high ball.

Although really an *arm caution,* while we're talking about *give* and the support needed to prevent it, hitters should also be aware of the fact that the *shoulder joints* also can give and, again, cause a weakening at contact. You know, it's funny — the skill of hitting is surrounded by talk that leads you to believe that it is one graceful, easy movement. But as you grow to understand it more, I'm sure you'll find it quite the contrary. After a swing decision, hitting becomes a *grunting skill,* a skill of aggression; something *fast and strong.* However, I never viewed it like that until I learned its correct execution. I mean, with poor mechanics I didn't hit the ball anywhere near as hard or as often. *It was the result of proper execution that changed my attitude toward the movements of this skill, building both my confidence and swing aggression. And it is a lack of knowledge, execution, and therefore confidence that causes the movements of this skill to be described differently than they really are.* Hitting isn't *flower picking*; it's got some guts to it, or as Ted would say, "some umph."

The Head and Eyes

Maybe I was brainwashed, but I didn't believe it. I didn't want to. And at first, you won't either. But you *do not* watch the ball hit the bat! I know you've heard it just as I have: "Keep your eye on the ball," but it's not completely true. In a hitting discussion with Ted, he mentioned that the head and eyes go toward the *anticipated* direction of the hit, implying that the hitter did not watch the ball to contact. Naturally, I questioned him further, and his conclusion was that you don't watch the ball all the way in. I then questioned the stories of Ted's eyes, *the greatest eyes in baseball*; the eyes that could see what stitch was hit, that could read revolving record labels, and could see the ball actually hit the bat. "That's all garbage," he answered. What Ted was claiming was that any hitter, himself included, sees the ball out in front of him

(tunneling), and if he does swing his head should rotate with the rest of his body. Though this sounds radical at first, it caught my attention because I always felt as though I was cutting my hip rotation short by keeping my head *in.* I also felt that when I dropped my eyes and head to try to see the ball better, ironically, I lost sight of the pitch. Looking back now, I realize that both my claims were true. Hey, your head is the *top axis* of your hip rotation. If you stick it down, you create a counter movement in your swing because everything else is rotating in the other direction. *Hitters that drop their heads lose speed, power, and time by cutting down hip action and therefore slowing their swings down.* As far as losing sight of the ball, I was on target there also. If a hitter drops his head, he *definitely loses sight* of the ball and then faces the dilemma of picking it up again and hitting it square. *Don't do it.* It's a hundred times harder.

The thing that really perked up my experimentation on this issue was a simple test that Ted used to convince me of his claim. He asked me to focus my sights on a sign about 60 feet away. After I did he then held his finger about four or five feet in front of me, a sure strike, a little lower than my letters. He said, "Okay. When I say 'now,' you look at my finger as quick as you can." When I did he confirmed, "See, it took you just a split second to refocus, didn't it?" When I agreed, the point became clear. How can anybody drop their head or eyes, causing them to lose sight, and then attempt to resight and focus on a moving object traveling 80 or 90 miles an hour, when they can't even do it with a stationary object? The answer is, it can't be done. It's impossible. Terry Bahill, a Carnegie-Mellon University Professor, declared "Keeping your eye on the baseball is physiologically impossible." Bahill, in a current study done with students, amateur players, and major league players, found that not one subject, even ones with exceptional motor skills, could track a baseball closer than six feet at ninety miles per hour. "Humans simply cannot track targets moving with such high angular velocities." The best hitters, he then theorized, aren't those who can track the flight of the ball from the pitcher to the bat, but those who correctly guess where the ball will be at the moment of contact.

As far as I'm concerned, when the ball gets to a certain point, you've got a choice; you can keep your head in, losing both sight of the ball and time, or you can rotate your head and eyes to where the ball should be hit, still losing sight of the ball but gaining time. I'll take the time. Using your head and entire body correctly with proper mechanics gives a hitter more time to see, therefore helping to keep *good pitches good* rather than making them *great* through the *sluggish eyes* of poor technique. Proper movement of the head is one more way of gaining time.

You can be sure I'm not going to close off here because Chapter 5 of Lau's book is entitled "Your Head Goes Down When You Swing." And I read the *Boston Globe* one Sunday in 1982 and they had Walt Heriniak (current Red Sox batting coach), on how to hit a baseball. And one of his helpful points was, "Your head goes down when you swing." I remember distinctly it was right alongside "You hit off your front foot."

Sure, on a low ball your head drops a little, but it drops while the ball is in the first half of its flight, and that's okay because you won't lose sight of it out there. When it comes time to hit that low pitch, however, your eyes and head will be on the way out. The head movement that makes me cringe and you less the hitter is demonstrated in Sequence 44a through 44c.

On a different note, I do feel it's important to have the head tilt in slightly to the plate *after* a hitter decides to swing because this will aid the hitter's balance and swing consistency. I feel the head should first tilt in and then go slightly up like everything else. Before the swing, however, the head will stay straight up and as still as possible. Good movement of the head can be seen in Sequence 45a through 45c. Notice at a certain point how the eyes have *changed direction*, along with the head tilted and looking toward the probable direction of the hit. Hey, if things are looking down, maybe you are. Use your head, and see what I'm talking about.

44a

44b

44c

This sequence demonstrates what I consider poor use of the head and eyes. Here, the head acts as a counter-movement to hip rotation while the eyes are expected to see what can't be seen.

45a

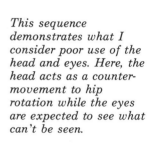

Here, after doing their initial job, the head and eyes continue to aid contact percentage by allowing the body to rotate freely, therefore maintaining its speed and consistency.

45b

45c

The Swing Plane Mystery

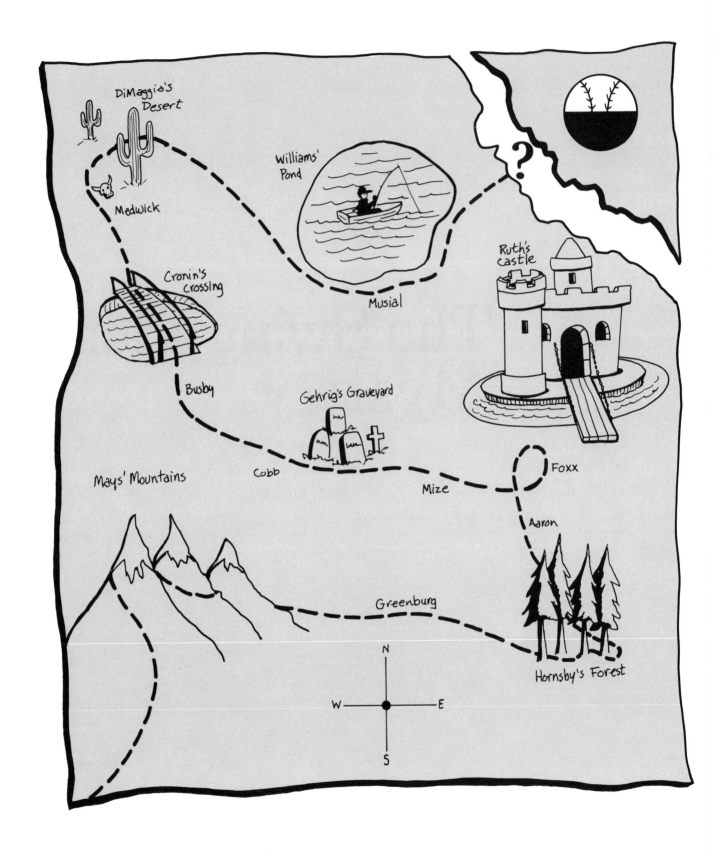

In front of hitting's common uncertainties one question dominates national hitting conversation, and that's in reference to the plane of the swing. How do you swing a bat at a baseball? Is it a down, level, or slight upswing?

Studying this particular mystery off and on for eight years, I wish to share with you a most interesting conclusion. The swing plane mystery stems from an undiscovered piece of information — a corner ripped off the hitting treasure map. Hey, aren't most mysteries caused by a lack of information? In the movies they never tell you that the butler is the murder victim's real father or that the gardener is a C.I.A. agent. This information doesn't come out until the end, and when you finally piece the connecting information in place many prejudged factors are then seen in a different light.

Before I identify the missing link and solve the swing plane mystery, I must first briefly review both the pros and cons of each individual plane as I have found them: on the field, in magazines, books, both teaching and learning, and also in general hitting conversation.

Looking first at the *slight upswing*, made popular by Ted in the "Science of Hitting," we find a theory that basically states, while the pitcher stands on a 10-inch mound and throws the ball from about ear level to an area around the hitter's knees (which most pitchers strive for), the ball is coming *down*, and therefore if a hitter wishes to increase his contact percentages by having his bat stay within the path of the oncoming ball for the longest period of time, he must swing slightly up in relation to the ground, making his swing level to the plane of the pitch. Diagram 12a denotes the plane of this swing.

Most critics of the slight upswing will *not* dispute the idea of swinging slightly up to increase the chances of hitting a ball coming slightly down. However, most will begin criticizing the slight upswing as being *ineffective*. For example, after a short explanation of the slight upswing, Lau comments "My confidence in the accuracy of this theory is considerably underminded by the fact that I have never seen anyone make it work." Later he goes on to claim that not even Williams swung up. Lau and most attackers of the slight upswing will also claim that when it does work,

it puts too many balls in the *air*, the air being viewed by many over the years as the easiest place to field a ball. They'll be quick to say that if the ball is bouncing on the ground, often bouncing crazily, it's a harder ball to field. Continuing on, they'll point out that, with the ball on the ground, the fielder has two jobs instead of one because now he must field and then still throw the runner out, as opposed to just simply catching the ball. Naturally, they conclude that balls hit on the ground can't help but lead to more errors, base runners, and runs scored.

Another popular attack made on the slight upswing is that it is not feasible for the fast runner — the guy who can fly down the line. The argument being that most of the runner's game is on the ground, with grounders up the middle and in the holes. Why should this hitter ever want to use an air-plagued slight upswing? They often summarize that the slight upswing is a swing only good for power hitters.

Hopping planes to the *downswing*, this hitter is swinging down in relation to both the oncoming plane of the ball and the ground.

Diagram 12b illustrates this swing. The major support of this theory is built not only upon the advantages of hitting the ball on the ground, but also on the idea that the downswing will very rarely, if at all, produce an *easy to field* pop-up or fly ball. Advocates of the downswing will claim that when it's executed properly it will produce both hard grounders and line drives. Downswing defendants also claim that balls hit off a downswing will possess an aiding backspin, causing line drives hit with the downswing to carry farther than when hit with either of the two competing strokes. Diagram 12c displays this spin.

Critics of the downswing will attack its very small potential contact area, claiming that its use cuts down the percentages of any type of contact — good or bad. As far as ground balls go, most will agree that the grounder can be a more difficult play; however, most do not believe that hitting the majority of your balls on the ground is a strong foundation for success. In a similar light to that of the slight upswing, critics will claim that the power hitter usually has *no game* on the ground, due to their usual size and speed. They then ask, "Why would the power hitter use a swing plagued with ground balls?"

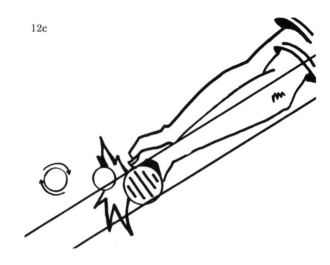

12c

The last and certainly the most popular of the three theories is the *level swing*. Before we review the level swing, however, please note that when I speak of level, I am referring to a swing traveling on a plane level to the *ground* (as illustrated in Diagram 12d). While the majority of level swing supporters define their swing as *level to the ground*, a small minority of them will confusingly claim their swing is traveling on a plane level to the ball, therefore, in my mind, then become slight upswing supporters.

12b

12d

Followers of the level swing build their case upon one major point — that the level swing will aid the hitter in hitting the center of the ball and a resulting line drive more often than the other two theories. Level swingers usually view the slightly up and downswings as *opposite extremes*, protesting that both are infested with an abundance of *off-centered contact*, causing the bat to hit either the top half of the ball in the downswing for a harvest of grounders, or the bottom half in the slight upswing for a herd of pops and flys.

Interesting in itself is that unlike the other theories, most level swing people believe their swing is the ideal swing, that is, the swing for all hitters regardless of style. They'll claim the level swing produces not only a reasonable percentage of fly balls for the power hitter, but also a reasonable percentage of ground balls for the runner.

Arguments against the level swing are not in abundance. Again, it is the most *popular swing*. However, slight upswing believers, as you might suspect, will claim that it could have a better potential contact zone, while downswingers will say it produces "too many balls in the air," along with the absence of that aiding backspin we spoke of. Still the question remains, "On which plane will your career ride?"

The missing clue to *the swing plane mystery* is what I call *the lighting effect*. You see, regardless of when or where you hit, the light is always *above*; and therefore, whether it's a sunny day, a cloudy day, an indoor batting cage or a night game, the *light* is always coming *down*. The result is a pitch where *the top of the ball is brighter than the bottom*. Because the light is coming down on a *nontransparent* sphere, the bottom *does not have the angle* to pick up as much light and therefore it is darker. *It's in the shade!* Also, keep in mind that the hitter is *looking down on* the pitch (most pitches are thrown at knee level).

What does this have to do with the plane of the swing? Unfortunately, even at the slowest speeds, where the two tones are easily detected, the top of the ball is more *attractive* to the hitter; and in the split second high pressured skill of hitting, the top of the ball lures the hitter to attack *it* rather than the *ball's center*. Going a step further, when we

increase the velocity to 80 or 90 miles an hour, the bottom of the ball can be *impossible* to see. At a high speed the lighting effect displays the top of the ball like a *neon sign*, catching both the hitter's attention and attack. Have you ever heard a hitter say that a pitcher was throwing *seeds, pills or BB's*? What they were experiencing was the optical illusion of the ball becoming smaller, when in reality it had only changed size in relation to their ability to *see it in its entirety*. Due to the lighting effect, hitters are only seeing and hitting the top half of the ball, as seen in Diagram 13a.

13a

Because the light source is above, the top of the ball is brighter. This has a major effect on the plane of the swing.

If you think about hitters seeing and attacking the top of the ball, it makes sense to assume that the most productive swing plane would be the plane that would *bring the hitter to the center* of the ball. The *level swing* has been that plane; it has brought the hitter to the center of the ball! However, the success of the level swing rests upon the *odd fact* that the plane of the pitch, coupled with the plane of the level swing, creates a tendency for contact to be made *under the target* the hitter sees and attempts to contact. Interesting enough is that the level swing will only bring a hitter to the center of the ball when the ball is coming *down*. Hypothetically, the hitter, using a level swing to contact a level pitch, would probably ground it out because now the *aiding* angular relation between the path of the pitch and the path of the swing would not bring his contact point on the ball *below* the original target. Remember, this hitter does *not realize* he is attacking the top of the ball. This hitter believes he is seeing a complete ball that looks small because it's going fast. These concepts can be seen in Diagrams 13b and 13c.

Now that hitters know the top of the ball is brighter, there is no need to rely on *circumstances* to get you to the center of the ball. Every hitter should create a new *target area* by thinking of hitting *under the white*, therefore bringing them to the ball's center logically. Now, you might ask, "Isn't that going to then bring you under the ball or to its bottom half?" And you'd be right, except that the ideal baseball swing is not a level swing! *The ideal baseball swing and the answer to the swing plane mystery is a slight upswing, where the hitter understands the lighting effect and thinks of getting under the white.*

Now that the hitter understands where the center of the ball is, he would be foolish to ignore the potential contact area of the slight upswing, not to mention the fact that it's the *only swing* that hits the ball *right smack on the nose*, utilizing all the available momentum. The other two swings tend to slice the ball, throwing valuable momentum out the window, especially the downswing. These concepts can be seen in Diagrams 13d and 13e.

13b

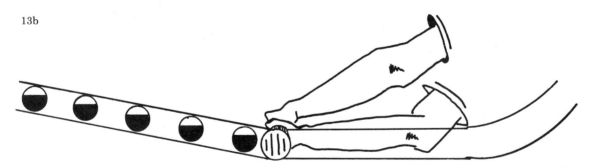

"Unaware" of the lighting effect, the level swing has "found" the center of a ball traveling "down".

13c

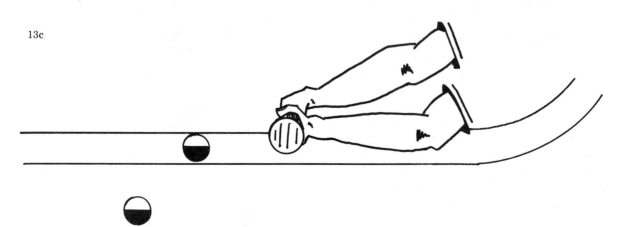

"Unaware" of the lighting effect, the level swinger would "ironically ground out" the level pitch.

13d

13e

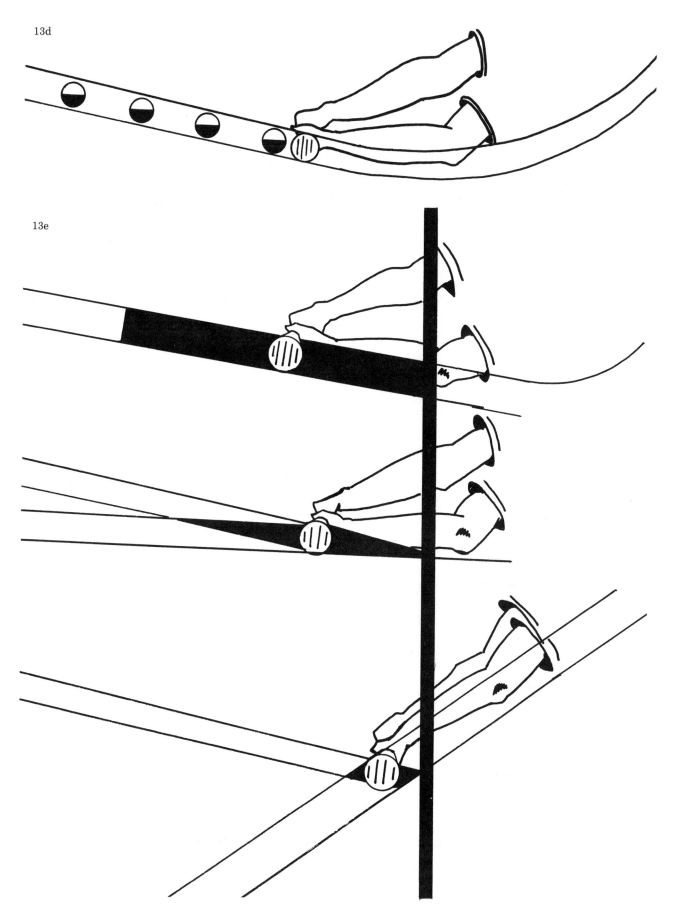

Disciple of a Master

13f

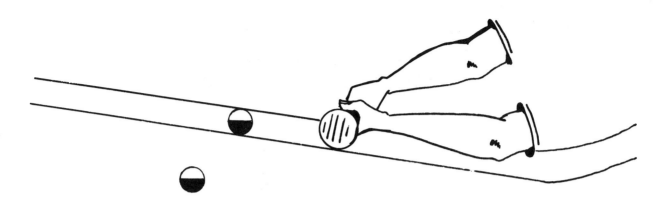

Much like a level swinger at a level pitch, the slight up swinger unaware of the lighting effect will ground out the ball that's coming down.

13g

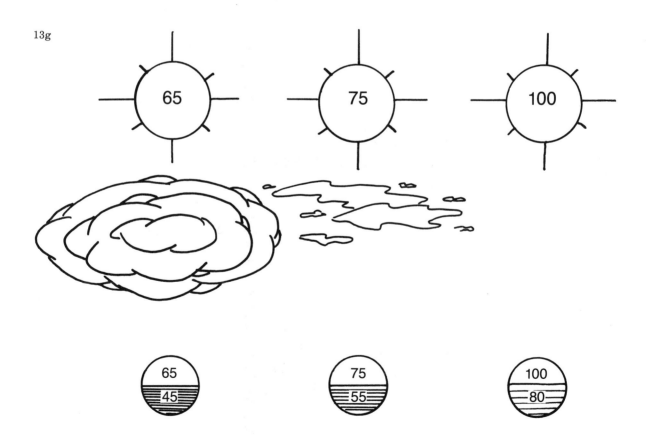

This diagram displays the days light and its effect on what you'll see. The brighter the day, the better.

As for the slight upswing putting too many balls in the air, that's crazy. Before my discovery of the lighting effect, I found it ironically to be *ground ball prone*. It's really simple to figure out. Though the plane of the swing was in line with the plane of the pitch, the target was still the top of the ball; the result much like the level swing at the level pitch is a ground ball. This is seen in Diagram 13f.

Also, the slight upswing is geared toward hitting *line drives*. If you imagine a ball hit from your belt buckle back through the pitcher's release point, that ball is going to be a line drive. Remember, the slight upswing is based on meeting the plane of the bat with the average plane of the ball. If the ball comes in at 8 to 10 degrees, good execution will send it back out on that same angle.

As for the downswing, I think it's *foolishness* because it barely has a potential contact area. Anybody that hits well swinging down could be way better than what they are. I will support the claim about the ball spinning and carrying. Sliced balls will carry, but they won't carry farther than a ball hit on the nose; *there is no comparison*. Also, line drives that are hit with downswings carry *slowly*, making them easier to field. A *hard* line drive to field is one with a *top spin* off the slight upswing because it will sink; or even worse, if you hit it *right on the nose*, it will knuckle.

While we're on the subject, do you see the ball better on a bright day or a gray day? Good question, isn't it? I pondered over this one for a long while and concluded that a bright day, a sunny day, was far better. After I realized that the top half of the ball was brighter, the next logical question to ask was, is the top half of the ball on a sunny day, brighter than the top half on a gray day? Naturally, the answer is yes. I feel the best way to think of lighting is like reading a book under different watt bulbs. The brighter the bulb, the clearer the print. The brighter the day, the clearer the ball — therefore making it easier to see and easier to hit. This is displayed in Diagram 13g.

I know. You want to know what to aim for if you're playing a game and the sun is setting, causing its light to shine from the side, as seen in Diagram 13h. Well, aim for the white, because in this case the ball's height, the key dimension in target area, is represented truly.

13h

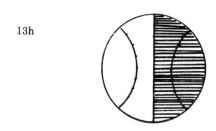

Sometimes, the sun will be setting and the ball will appear like this. Here, the ball's height is represented truely, so aim for the white.

Style Is Not Technique

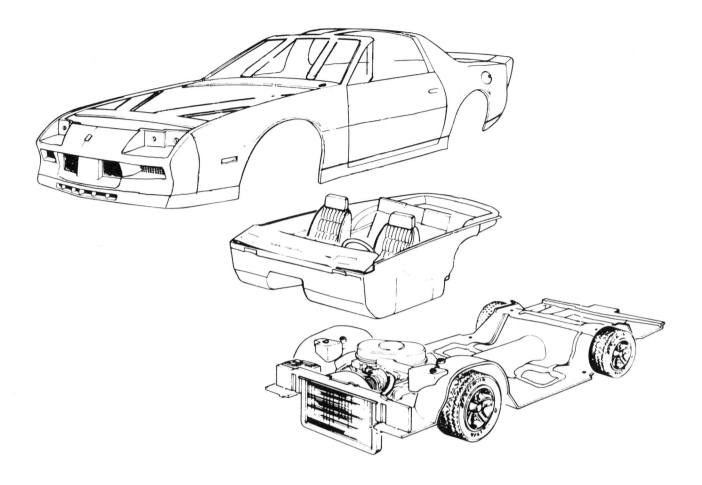

If I could correct only one flaw in hitting today, I would unquestionably choose to individually define the terms *style* and *technique*. The reason I say this is because today these words are viewed to mean the same, but are really very different. The distinction between style and technique lies in the fact that *style* is personal and *technique* is universal. That is to say that style is an *individual* aspect of hitting, where technique should be basically the same for everyone. Of the two words, technique is not the word that's being misinterpreted. It is a *method* or an *approach* to a task. Style, however, is very different. Although an unavoidable aspect of hitting and a distinct feature of proper technique, style is *not* technique, but rather the *direction* in which the hitter *must utilize* his technique in order to reach potential.

When I refer to style as utilizing technique in a productive direction, I am viewing style as an *offensive position* or an *offensive role*. Naturally, the correct role or style to play is

simply the one that will be most productive in relation to your talent. Think about it, if Danny Ainge and Larry Bird ran, shot, and dribbled with the same *basic techniques* (which they probably do), could they switch positions? Of course not. The reason prohibiting this would simply be an insufficient *genetic makeup* for the demands of the new style or role. Although Ainge and Bird may make the same bodily movements to run, shoot, and dribble, one will be faster, taller, stronger, more aggresive, and so on, therefore altering his individual capability and placing his *potential* in the rhelm of one role or style as opposed to another. Sad as it is, *style is governed by talent!*

The confusion between style and technique has grown thick due to the popular belief that style is something you *create*; when in reality it is something you must *realize*. The direction, role, or style that you should adopt can only be found through a hard and honest look at your strengths and weaknesses. It's not so difficult to understand. It's like building a model car: you're not *making the parts*, you're putting them together the *only* way they'll look best. Obviously, an honest evaluation is the key.

If you dream up make-believe parts for your car and continue to build upon them, sooner or later you'll face the sad realization that something is drastically out of place; and now with the glue long dry, the possibility of reaching top shelf will be gone.

"Hit according to your style," Williams warned. However, like so many other statements in hitting, this statement has been misinterpreted. People have twisted it and continued to twist it to mean *hit the way you want*; that is, invent your own technique and call it *your style*. I see and hear this all the time and it's cutting potential hitters, the skill of hitting, and baseball to ribbons. It's placing the complex execution of how to hit a baseball on the shoulders of the young athlete and naturally, he can't handle it. Consequently, we're faced with confusion, frustration, and worst of all, *lasting faith* in personal sub-par hitting techniques justified as style.

With a basic understanding of style, it's very important to zero in on your style and the realization of it. Style is a complex part of hitting and reaching potential *demands* that every hitter find and utilize his own style correctly. To simplify this let's break style into two parts: *basic style* and *individual style*.

While it is true that each hitter holds his *own style*, it is also true that hitters and their styles (like Ainge and Bird) can be placed into *basic categories*. Surely, we've all heard of *power hitters* and *singles hitters*, just like we've heard of *guards* and *forwards*. Terms like power hitter or singles hitter, although vaguely defined, suggest two distinct directions or roles that hitters have followed in the past and will continue to follow in the future. Although I feel the categories or names you commonly hear such as; power hitter, singles hitter, opposite field hitter or "Punch-n'-Judy" convey inaccurate connotations, I strongly believe that similar but better defined categories would be extremely helpful to the teaching, learning and understanding of the skill.

To aid this belief, I have identified and defined three different hitting categories that clearly reflect the hitter's intended role, position or direction. I call these categories *basic style categories*, or a hitter's basic style.

A hitter's basic style is the groundwork or platform from which he will launch his technique best, consequently discovering basic style should be approached with painstaking care. The truth is never simple, nor is this. Here the hitter must *honestly* self-analyze and evaluate his *major* strengths and weaknesses: for example, his attitude, intelligence, footspeed, quickness, power, coordination, and courage. Then, after he has passed an honest judgment upon himself, he must match his capabilities with the demands of a fitting basic style and begin to explore it. Here are those categories.

The Pull Hitter

The hardest hitting style is the pull hitting style. As a right-handed batter, this hitter hits the ball most of the time between the left field line and the second baseman. This hitter bats in an *even* stance, making his general contact area much closer to the pitcher than the other two styles. This factor cuts down both his reaction time and margin of contact error. Consequently, the pull hitter *must* be quick with the bat.

The pull hitter should also be a long ball threat — he must be capable of consistently creating enough momentum to *potentially* put any speed pitch in the seats (that is, any pitch that *should* be pulled). Although a requirement of all three basic styles, the pull hitter must be *extremely* smart, selective, patient and observant, as he will be pitched to very carefully and therefore, must prepare for and read pitches very well.

The Middle Man

The most common hitting style should be hitting up the middle. This right-handed batter hits balls from the short stop—third base hole to the second base—first base hole. The middle man bats from a *slightly closed* stance, creating a contact area farther from the pitcher than the pull hitter, therefore establishing more reaction time. The middle man may or may not be a long ball threat; if he is, he will also be pitched to carefully and therefore must also be very smart, patient, observant and selective. It is a plus if he's a relatively fast runner, as his contact area will cause many balls to be hit up the middle and to the outfield gaps. However, this is not imperative.

The Singles Hitter

This hitter is *extremely fast*. He has the ability to beat out any difficult infield play; therefore, his strength is in making contact. For contact assurance this hitter uses a shortened swing (will elaborate). He also hits up the middle as described for the middleman.

The singles hitter also must be very patient because he will be *made to hit*. Again, a .300 hitter fails seven out of ten times. And because singles hitters are *not* long ball threats, the tendency is to go right at them, which can also lead to overaggressiveness and poor pitch selection.

If you understand the significance of each basic style category and have the ability to honestly self-evaluate your talent areas, then you will probably be able to find the basic style that fits you best. When you do, then you must take it on to the field to confirm your choice. Take your time. The general hitting areas for each style can be seen in diagrams 14a and 14b.

The Stride (Its purpose and starting time)

The purpose of the following sections are to convey *why, when, how,* and *where* you should stride. Though the stride's association with the stretch position alone confirms its mechanical prominence, it's entanglement with style, timing, and the overall quality of the swing demands a more detailed explanation. Due to the stride's central position in the chain of hitting's mechanics, a strong understanding of the following material should not only enrich your present approach, but also help with the ongoing chore of correction and adjustment.

There is no way you can understand stride's importance or it's execution until you first understand its purpose. Why do hitters stride? Basically, hitters stride for one reason, and that is *to gain preliminary body momentum before and during the hitter's decision to swing.* The hitter uses his stride like a *headstart.* That is to say, he uses it to get his body moving before he actually *knows* what or

14a

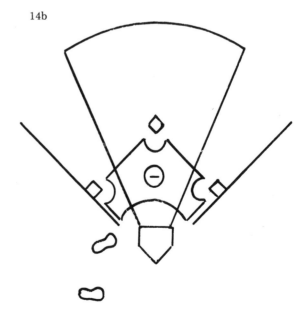

14b

14a shows the area in which the "pull hitter" hits. As a right handed batter, it ranges from the left field line to the second baseman.

14b displays the area in which both the "middle man" and "singles hitter" hit. It ranges from the short stop-third base hole to the second base-first base hole.

where the pitch is, and therefore whether he wishes to swing or not. By moving the body (breaking inertia) before his decision, the hitter will not have to *waste time* getting his body moving after a decision to swing. Therefore, when timed properly, this preliminary body momentum (or headstart) provides the hitter with more time.

Getting the body moving early is the goal, and it is a great advantage. Think about it. If you were jogging and then suddenly decided to burst into a sprint, that first sprinting step would be much easier than from a dead start because you were already moving. I mean, you didn't have to *start* the movement, you merely *increased* it. Stride does the same thing for the hitter — it primes and therefore enhances your swing.

With our purpose in mind, the starting time of the stride becomes critical. Though I said earlier that the ideal starting time was when the pitcher's arm came over his throwing shoulder, it's really the *lower arm* that marks the starting point. The hitter should start to stride before the high speed extention of the pitcher's forearm and wrist starts toward the plate. The hitter is clearly *starting* his stride *before the ball has been released*, and that must be understood. If the hitter starts striding after the release point, or even during the release point, he is *late* — he's behind the ball because he's behind with his movements and, as a result, his headstart advantage is then forfeited. The ideal starting time can be seen in Photo 46a.

I have found hitters at all levels to be late striding and foolishly handing away a good portion of their potential success. In a sample of 400 hitters at the little league, pony league, and high school level, I found 90 percent of the little league level, 72 percent of the pony league level, and 63 percent of the high school level to be late striding. I have also found late striding to still be a major problem at both the college and professional levels. Proper stride timing is a simple mechanic that every hitter should master. However, many times hitters with both fine swings and attitudes will go through their careers being less than what they could have been simply because they didn't know *how to stride on time*. It's sad. It's like practicing a piano solo and then starting it a measure late every concert. All the

Here, my brother Rick helps convey the starting point of both the cocking motion and the stride (stretch position).

46a

hard work you've done on your solo (your swing) is depressingly soured because the solo can only be dynamic if it comes in at the correct time. Certainly, the good hitters don't miss their cue. As much as I've disagreed with Lau's work, he conducted a great film study on the 1980 All-Star game that showed every hitter starting his stride before the ball had been released. *No one* was dead late striding the entire game. Why then is late striding such a problem?

Late Striding

The causes behind late striding are more than interesting. For example, though stride can be easily taught through good instruction, it can be extremely hard to learn on your own. Unfortunately, any hitter that begins to learn good stride timing faces a *fear* — a fear of committing his body *somewhat* without *any* pitch information. The hitter is afraid of swinging too early. *(Swinging early holds a place of horror in every hitter's mind. The early swing usually succeeds in making a spectacle of the hitter in a broken-down, half-hearted display. It is hitting's highest plateau of mechanical embarassment and therefore feared the most.)* Therefore, though the stride movements themselves are fairly simple, a hitter trying to learn them on his own without any *feedback* or *reinforcement* may never overcome that fear of commiting early and therefore never learn stride timing correctly (especially if he's under pressure). Naturally, the younger the hitter, the greater the fear.

Another interesting cause is due to the overall misconception that you must see the ball and then hit it. Sure, you've got to see the ball to hit it, but the connotation has become to see the ball and then move, and that is not the way it's done. You do not have to see the ball before you move. I get irritated when I hear a coach use the popular saying, "see the ball, hit the ball," because I know many kids will misunderstand and, as a result, stride late. Better sayings would be "move, see, and hit" or "stride, see, and hit," because these sayings are a truer reflection of the task. On the other hand, as much as I hate this misconception, I can fully understand it. I mean, *initially* you would think that it's much smarter to see the ball before you start your stride, especially knowing that the pitcher can throw different pitches. Certainly, it sounds more logical than stepping out there without *any information.* But the fact of the matter is that *it is impossible to hit in that fashion with consistency and authority.* The ball is just traveling too fast in relation to moving your *body* in time. Sure, you might be late and get a *piece* with your *wrists* and *arms*, but that's not hitting, that's just contact. Hitting and contact are two different things. Remember, hitting is a full body effort and if we expect the larger body parts to contribute and be positioned correctly at contact we've got to get them *warmed up* before we call on them to perform.

There is also a *visual factor* that has caused late striding. Regardless of the sport, it is often very difficult to notice a relationship between two body movements, like that found between the pitcher's arm and the start of the stride. Remember, these movements are taking place at the same time, 45 to 60 feet apart. Therefore, to see the relation between these movements, the observer must be behind either the pitcher or the hitter *with both movements in view.* Many times coaches are positioned poorly to teach stride timing. Hey, whether your teaching a mechanic in hitting or someone to play the fiddle, if you can't see what's going on, how can you find faults, or correct them? You can't. And that's just what's happening. This simple mechanic is not understood or taught the way it should be.

Again, late striding occurs at all levels, but it starts at the pre-little league level. Pre-little league success is *pampered* by extremely slow pitching — pitching that is so slow it doesn't require a stride timing for contact. As a result, the kid's first impression of hitting is to see the ball and then get moving, rather than to get moving and then see the ball. Sure enough, as you might have experienced, when the kid gets to *little league*, the days of *see it and then get moving* are gone. The kid is suddenly faced with the *new task* of catching up to very fast pitching without the aid of stride timing. Obviously, he's dead meat. I was.

When I teach a young kid (a pre-little leaguer) I increase the size of the ball — I don't decrease the velocity. I use soft balls or very small playground balls thrown close to little league speed. Then, after the boy understands both the execution and importance of stride timing, I progress him by gradually decreasing the size of the ball. By teaching in this manner, I can take away fear of both *injury and failure* and teach stride timing at a speed close to the little league's. Why do I teach this way? Because the size of the ball (or target) is secondary to the understanding of stride timing, and the *first* thing a hitter must begin to learn is *how* and *when* he must move to hit an object moving at that kind of speed.

The hard part of hitting at this age centers around landing the stride on time in relation to the moving object. Can't most nine- and ten-year-olds hit a ball off a tee? Sure they can. And why? Because it's a simple task of hand-eye coordination. Kids are using and improving their hand-eye skills every day in a thousand different ways. Don't believe it? Draw a chalk line horizontally on a football dummy and have 100 nine-year-olds try to hit it with a very thin dowel. That's pretty fine hand-eye coordination, wouldn't you say? I'll bet they'll do much better than you thought.

Bet them a candy bar and they'll hit it in four tries (average). But place them against little league speed with a bat and a ball that are *10 to 15 times the circumference* of the chalk line or dowel and with poor stride timing they might not make *contact* in twenty-five cuts. Why? Because the thick of the task is *timing,* and good timing begins with starting the stride on time (I will expound).

With this in mind, I've got to ask, why take the timing out of a beginner's experience? Why have the pre-little leaguer hit slow pitching, or even worse hit off a tee? Granted, on the average a boy that age can't hit a baseball thrown at little league speed, and surely you can't increase the size of the ball as I do because they couldn't field it or throw it in a game situation. However, if a bat was invented at the proper weight, with a circumference at the meat end twice the size of a baseball, you could essentially get the same results in practice and in games as I do when teaching. The pre-little leaguer could experience the importance of stride and it's timing *with success,* due to the bat's enlarged circumference.

Obviously, you'd need someone that could pitch consistently. Maybe the coach could pitch for his team, which would not only help to find the bats of some of the other team's hitters, but also be in a better position to coach his kids on the field. Maybe some of the younger little league pitchers could get some control work throwing at a slower speed. Maybe the umpire could pitch.

Beginning hitters growing in this setting would make the jump to little league much easier. Plus, those pre-little league games would be more exciting, more interesting, *with more hit balls, base running, and defense.* Kids would be getting the experience they should get at that age, and there's no better time to learn.

Stride Movements

At the very beginning of the stride, as the body starts to rock forward and part into the stretch position, we see two main movements: the entire body *rocking forward* and the *parting* movement of the upper and lower bodies to the stretch position. Breaking down the movements of the stretch position, we find the lower body movement (the opening of the stride leg from the hip joint) controlled by the muscles of the *hip joint*, and that's important. Remember, the leg opens in the *same position* it held in the cocking motion as seen in Photos 47a and 47b. Meanwhile, the upper body movement (the shoulder turning back) is controlled by the rotative muscles in the *waist area*, as seen in Photos 48a and 48b. Therefore, both movements of the stretch position are initiated by *muscle*.

47a 47b

48a 48b

The above photos show the separate movements of the stretch position. Please note that both of these movements are initiated by muscles. The front leg opens from the hip, while the upper body rotates back from the waist.

The rocking of the body forward (the forward swing of the pendulum), however, is *not initiated by muscle*, but is rather the result of the body's position in the cocking motion. If the front shoulder and knee have turned in and down and there is more weight on the back foot than on the front foot, the *lifting* of the stride leg will cause the body to come forward due to *gravity*. In Photo 49a the peak of the cocking motion reveals how the stride leg is holding back a pending forward force due mainly to the position of the shoulders. As you can predict, when the hitter lifts and begins to open his stride leg, he will automatically begin to *fall* toward his balance point.

Due to the position of the shoulders, in 49a, the peak of the cocking motion reveals how the stride leg is holding back a pending forward force. As you can predict when the hitter lifts and begins to open his stride leg, gravity will cause him to "fall" toward the balance point.

Unfortunately, many times hitters will open their stride leg without rocking forward to balance. This should *not* be considered striding because if the hitter does not reach the *balance point*, he will have too much weight on the back foot and, as a result, less hip action when it comes time to swing. *The stride is both the opening of the front leg and the forward swing of the pendulum to balance.* The hitter is *opening* his stride leg while his body *falls* to the balance point.

You're dying to ask me, aren't you? You've been following right along closely and something sounds confusing. If the stride is a part of the stretch position, how can I claim that it provides the hitter with a *headstart*, when the upper body is supposed to be traveling in the *opposite* direction? A logical question. If we can flashback to the toy train parallel, you'll remember that the engine was heavier than the boxcar. Well, the hips and legs, like the toy engine, are also heavier and therefore have produced more momentum *forward* with the stride than the upper body has created going *back*. Once the connecting muscles are stretched and the body halves reach the stretch position, the hips, like the engine, will *overpower* the upper body and tow it along like the boxcar. The upper body *starts* back, but stops and then *redirects* in the direction of the hips.

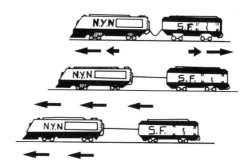

Much like the boxcar, the upper body starts back, but stops and then redirects forward.

The confusion that often arises stems from the fact that this all happens *during the flight of the stride*. While the foot is in the air (*before it lands*), the entire body will reach the stretch position and then, while in the stretch position, follow the path of the hips. Diagram 15a runs through the relation between the upper and lower body during the flight of the stride.

66

Starting with Frame 1, we see the cocking motion with the upper body (shoulders) and lower body (hips) represented with lines. Progressing to Frame 2, we watch the beginning of the stride where the hips and shoulders begin to travel apart. Frame 3 shows the hitter in the stretch position at about mid-flight; and at this point the shoulders will *not go back any further* — they have stopped while the hips continue to pull forward. Frame 4 shows the hips overpowering and pulling the upper body with it.

Answering the question, you can now see that the upper body moves back only so long before the hips pull the entire body forward, establishing the hitters headstart *before* the landing of the stride foot.

Though it's a very slight movement, you should also note that a hitter's headstart ends up in a *circular pattern.* I mean, if we're going to swing in a circular pattern, it only makes sense that our headstart should prime the same pattern, and it does. Towards the end of the stride's flight, after the body has reached the stretch position and the hips have started to turn the entire body with them, the body will start trying to turn the corner just slightly, and this turning movement will continue throughout the landing of the stride. This is denoted by the large arrow in Frame 4.

Also, the student should note that this *circular start* is a major responsibility of the *opening — the rotating of the stride leg.* A stride leg that does not *open*, but merely strides forward (a common problem), will do nothing for a circular headstart.

Stride Direction

We can't forget direction. Where does the stride go? Is it in toward the plate? Back to the pitcher? Parallel to the ball? Where do you stride? Before we talk about the *main direction* of the stride, it's important to first talk about its direction solely *in relation to the back foot.* Regardless of the hitter's basic style and stance, the stride should land and mark the third point on an extended line that runs from the hitter's back heel through his front heel as seen in Diagram 16. Note also that the even stance and closed stance both stride on the line I have just described, even though their main direction is different.

Why this heel line? Creating and striding upon this line is merely another precaution taken to assure the hitter of proper hip rotation. If you rotate your feet from this line, they will line up beneath and on the body side of the hip that they are supporting, providing a well-balanced base and therefore enabling the hitter to tap his maximum range of circular motion and potential rotative momentum. This is seen in Photos 50a-c. On the contrary, if the heels do not line up, the hitter may find that his front leg is cutting his hip rotation short. Due to the base he has created with his stride, his back leg will actually start to bind against his front leg in the crotch area, slowing down his swing and inhibiting his range of motion. Photos 51a-c display the results of a poorly aligned base caused by a stride that has gone off the heel line.

15a

Landing	Mid-Stride	Stretch	Cocking

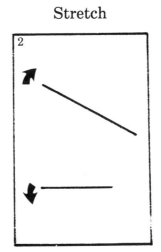 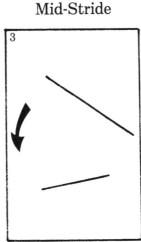  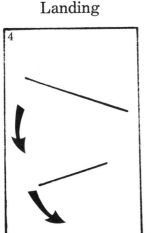

16

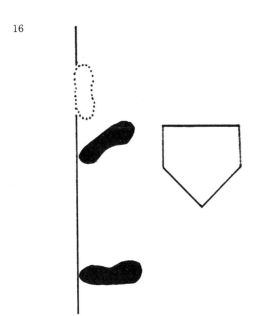

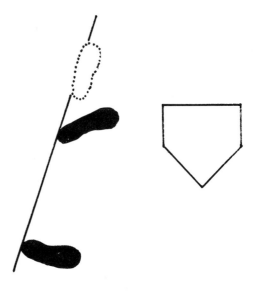

50a

50b

51a

51b

50c

Striding on the heel line assures good hip rotation allowing the feet to stably align beneath the hip they are supporting.

51c

The hitter that crosses the heel line, not only cuts his hip rotation short, but, will also feel unbalanced due to a narrowed base.

Also important, in Diagram 17 you can see that these two different hitters have their back feet forming a right angle to their heel line. Though I said earlier (when talking about stance) that the back foot lies straight across, it's really *perpendicular* (at 90°) *to the heel line*. The front foot's opened position (at about 45°) is also *only open* in relation *to the heel line*. Due to the open front foot, if the feet are positioned correctly in the stance, the front toe will be slightly *behind* the back toe when compared to a line drawn parallel to the heel line. This is seen in Diagram 18.

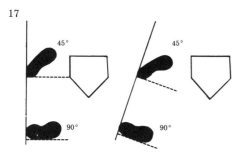

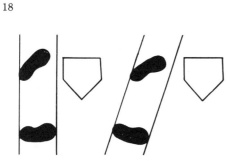

After your feet are starting and moving well in relation to each other, your next question is in reference to the main direction of your stride. Is it in? Out? Parallel? Where? As you may have figured, if we are going to stride upon the heel line, the stride must go in the direction that the heel line is pointing. So the real question becomes, *"How do you stand?"* rather than *"Where do you stride?"* And again, we're back to basic style. Once you select your basic style you must then realize that the direction in which the heel line is pointing will create your general contact area and therefore dictate the area in which you will hit the ball onto the field. This is why I identi-

fy both stance and stride as distinct elements of *style*. Before any confusion starts, I am *not* claiming that the direction of your stride is the direction that you'll hit the ball. Remember, a *pull* hitter's heel line is pointing toward *center field*, but he's not hitting the bulk of his balls up the middle; just as a right-handed *middleman* is pointing more toward the *second baseman's position*, but he's hitting the majority of his balls in the *middle* of the field. The reason is simply because the hips have the mobility to rotate *much further* to the left or right (depending on your batting side) than the direction of the stride. With a *right-handed* hitter in mind, the relation between the direction of his stride and where the majority of his balls will be hit is much like an *army tank* with it's nozzle stuck slightly to the left. If you line the tank up straight, it will be shooting like a pull hitter hits; and if you close or angle the tank off slightly, it will be shooting up the middle. Both can be seen in Diagram 19. Please note that there's a relation between how you stand, stride, and where the ball will go — and it's very important.

Certainly, I'm not saying anything *new*, hitters have been adjusting their feet and/or strides to direct the ball ever since the first hack. It's a natural tendency. However, it's time to take a good look at the pros and cons of these adjustments.

For example, take the guy who sets up in an *even stance* and then strides *in* like a middleman would. He's hurting himself. He is trying to *open* his stride leg while he steps *in*. Unfortunately, these clashing movements cause a poor circular headstart and its result tends to gear the hitter's swing toward only outside pitches. This hitter's stance and stride is seen in Diagram 20. On the other hand, what about the guy who sets up as a middleman, and then steps out to an even stride? I don't like him either. Though his movement is more natural because it's on the path of the swing, he is conversely gearing himself for inside pitches. Couple stepping out with the length of the bats used today and it really makes little sense. This hitter is seen in Diagram 21. I'm against any lateral stride movement — stay on the heel line.

19

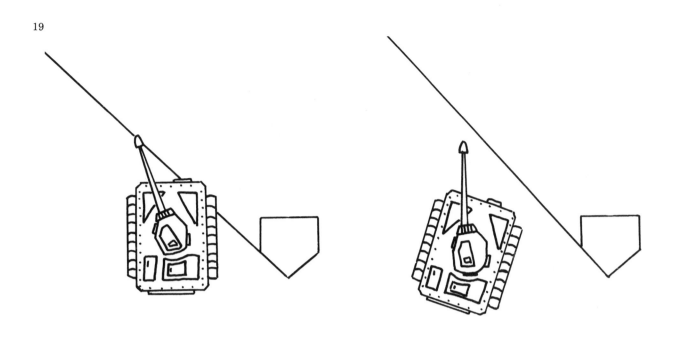

Because the hips have the ability to rotate beyond the angle of the heel line, the relation between the direction of the heel line and where the balls will be hit onto the field is much like an Army tank with its nozzle pointing slightly to the left.

20   21

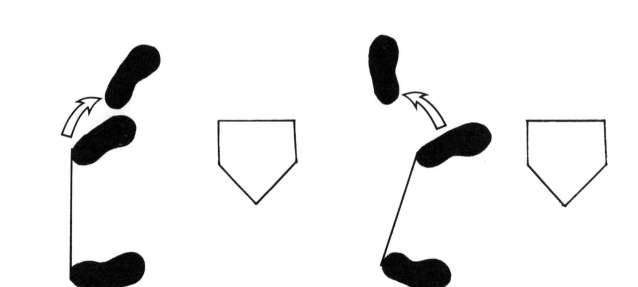

D20 displays the hitter who set up in an even stance and then breaks the heel line by stepping in. D21 shows the even stance hitter breaking the heel line by stepping out. I don't advise either. Stay on the heel line.

Style Stride and the Bottom Arm

Ya, I know. Pull hitter Ted Williams did *not* bat from an even stance, he batted from one that was *slightly* closed and, naturally, that goes against my basic style description of a pull hitter. Well, hear this, I don't think Williams used his arms as well as he could have. From the films and photos I've seen, he pre-extended them a little, and as I said earlier, this caused his average ball to be hit more to the right. Hey, the stories about Williams pulling the ball are endless: pulling in spite of the shift, pulling foul, and pulling into the Fenway bullpen. And while it's amazing how great a pull hitter Ted was, in my opinion (and I'm sure in his), he pulled the ball too much for his own good. Ted Williams was *not* a natural left-hander (he threw right-handed). And while most people know that, even the best don't really understand why it is such a *disadvantage*. Beyond the undesired inconvenience of not having the strongest, quickest, and most skilled arm on the top, closer to contact (which would have made Williams quicker, stronger, and more accurate), is the fact that by having his best arm on the bottom he was constantly drawn toward *pre-extension*. By having his *doing arm* (the arm that has always been most productive) on the bottom, Ted wanted to use it more than his top arm, making it very difficult for him to *anchor it properly*. Hey, bat from the other side someday, you'll feel what I'm talking about. It's a hard thing to deal with. *To me, there's no wonder at all as to why Ted had so much trouble going to the opposite field because the swing hitters used to get the ball up the middle and to the opposite field — the inside-out stroke, which we'll talk about in a moment, requires the hitter to keep both the arms bent throughout the entire swing.*

Where is all this leading to? The point is that whenever *pre-extension* is present, even if it's not that bad (as in Ted's case), there must be an alteration of *stance* and *stride* if the hitter is to hit the ball where he should. Ted Williams batted from a slightly closed stance to keep a reasonable percentage of his balls from going foul. *What hitters must understand is that there is an important relationship between the execution of the bottom arm, stance, stride, and style.* The more you extend, the more you'll pull the ball and the more you'll have to close off your stance and stride to put the ball where you should.

As we mentioned earlier, the problem stems from the angle on which the bat will approach the ball from a pre-extended swing and, unfortunately, the only way to solve this problem is by anchoring that front arm correctly. The *last thing a hitter wants to do is to accept* his pre-extension and try to combat it by altering his stance and stride. The hitter that tries this is merely robbing Peter to pay Paul. But you know, they're a dime-a-dozen on TV — big, strong guys pulling the ball with toothpick bats from extremely closed stances set way off the plate. A hitter like this that concedes to his pre-extension will not only have to pay *its* stiff and constant tolls (as discussed earlier), but will usually be forced to buy extra time with an extremely light and usually short bat.

Just as popular and twice as bad is when pre-extension dictates a hitter's *style*. Many times TV will feature a hitter that should clearly be a middleman, who's pulling the ball due to pre-extension. *This guy is miles away from his potential.* He's out of style, and he's pre-extending. What could be worse?

Not everybody is going to use their bottom arms as well as they should and therefore, although two middlemen are standing and striding on the same angle, one hitter may, on the average, pull the ball a bit more, that is to say that this hitter's hitting area will be slightly more to the pull side. If Hitter A pre-extends just slightly, on the average, he will pull the ball a bit more than Hitter B. *Please remember, however, that Hitter A is feeling the pains of slight pre-extension and therefore, if all talents are equal, Hitter B would be the better hitter.*

If Ted had been a natural lefty and did not pre-extend, he would have been even better. Mechanically, things would have been much easier for him. Had he used a longer bat and swung more efficiently, he would have hit balls harder, been quicker inside, hit less fouls, and hit the outside of the plate much harder. Just hitting the outside low corner more efficiently alone would have made him notably better because that's where everybody tried to pitch him. Fearing for their lives, pitchers would have started coming in on him more often (pull hitters hit a good percentage of outside pitches up the middle). Also, just due to the fact that he would not have been pulling as *many* balls, the *shifts* he faced would never have come about.

Now, don't get me wrong — *I think Ted was the best.* However, I don't think he was mechanically to his potential, and I'm not sure anyone ever has been to theirs. I know, how can I claim someone as great as Ted Williams had a mechanical drawback? Well, let me ask you a question for a change. "Are greats always executing to their potential?" Logic tells me that they are not. I've seen films of Willie Mays hitting, and the first thing that came to mind was how much better he could have been with better mechanics. Willie had a very long stride which only placed his legs in a lesser position at crunch time. As we've discussed, this took a bite out of contact percentage. Again, please don't misunderstand. I'm not downing him. He may very well be the greatest all-around baseball player to ever step on the field. I just want you to know that I don't like this *leave-the-guy-alone syndrome* just because he's good. I think Willie Mays is a great example of someone who lost out because the coach was *afraid* to take a shot at helping him reach his potential. *"Don't argue with success"* and *"Leave well enough alone"* are attitudes that greats are constantly faced with. I think it stinks.

I don't think Willie was too fond of that attitude either. I saw him on a late night talkshow one time, and I detected resentment. He implied that he knew he could have been better. He said *"No one ever taught me anything. They just sent me out there."*

The Speed of the Stride: Timing

There is no better spot to begin defining another popular but misted hitting concept, and that's *timing*. All my baseball life I've heard or read baseball authorities claim that this skill was *all timing*, but never have I heard one explain exactly what they meant. What is timing? Where, when, and how do you time a pitch?

The bulk of a hitter's timing lies in his ability to get the speed of his stride (his falling forward) to jell with the speed of the anticipated pitch in such a way that will enable the hitter to "fluently" reach his point of balance, decide upon the pitch and, if desired, continue harmoniously into his swing. Timing's main focus is *timing the balance point*, and this takes place in *the pre-swing*.

Let's face it, timing is not in the speed of your swing. I mean, you shouldn't swing *faster* to catch up to a fast ball or *slower* to wait on a curve. Your swing speed is one of hitting's few constants, and it should remain the same for all pitches. However, if both the swing speed and starting time of the stride remain consistent, how can you time different speed pitches smoothly? You know as well as I do if you were to stride and swing the same way for a curve traveling 60 miles per hour and a fast ball traveling 90 miles per hour, you would be anything but *fluent*. And why? Because the timing of one stride and one balance point *can't* accommodate all speed pitches. Therefore, we can conclude that if the hitter wishes to swing at a given pitch from a balance point that is *on time* rather than a balance point that has arrived too *early* or *late*, the hitter, like the pitcher, must have the ability to fluctuate his timing, that is, to alter the arrival time of his balance point in relation to the speed he is anticipating. How is this done?

Timing your balance point is controlled by *offsetting* certain amounts of weight in the *cocking motion* to slow down or increase the *speed* of the stride. For example, if I were anticipating a 60-mile-an-hour curve ball, I would bring *more weight back* in the cocking motion than I would if I were anticipating a 90-mile-an-hour fastball because the added offset of weight back would *decrease the speed* in which my body would *rock or fall* forward. Therefore, if I had calculated correctly, this offset of weight would then bring me to my balance point while the anticipated pitch was at the distance where I could handle its speed best. Conversely, anticipating the 90 mile-an-hour pitch, I would have offset *less weight back*, causing my stride (my body) to fall forward *faster*, enabling me to reach the balance point *sooner* and again while the pitch was at the distance where I could handle its speed best. By adjusting the weight distribution in the cocking motion, the hitter will alter the speed of his stride and therefore time his balance point in relation to the anticipated velocity.

The movement that offsets weight in the cocking motion is the *bending of the back leg*. To offset weight in the cocking motion the hitter merely bends the back leg *straight down* to a degree that will bring the proper amount of weight back in relation to the pitch he is anticipating. This can be seen while anticipating two different speeds (Photos 52a and b).

52a   52b

With this in mind, we can also conclude that the size of the pendulum also fluctuates in relation to the anticipated pitch. If a hitter goes further back for a slower pitch he creates a greater swing of the pendulum. On the other hand, the anticipation of a faster pitch will produce a shorter pre-swing.

Pendulum at Two Speeds

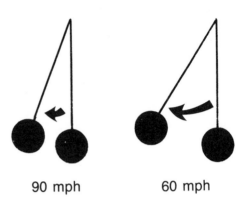

90 mph   60 mph

The anticipation of a slower pitch creates a greater backward and forward swing of the pendulum.

To calculate a weight shift you must have estimated and remembered about how fast the anticipated pitch was traveling. Where do you get this information? Again, you've *observed*. You've taken a pitch and you've questioned the hitters that have already faced the pitcher. You're taking in information and then storing it — storing it in an *ongoing file* of experience that eventually enables you to realize exactly how much weight you must offset to handle the different speed pitches you'll face, not only on that day but throughout your career. The smart hitter remembers not only the speeds and the timings of them, but also what pitchers throw them. By doing this, the hitters task of day-to-day timing becomes much easier because pitchers start to fall into categories. I mean, White, Rogers, and Farley may have similar speed fast balls and/or curves, and by knowing this from past experience the smart hitter will be able to formulate a timing advantage before he ever steps into the batter's box. *When he does get in the box, however, he'll still strictly observe because he knows it's very possible that "this time" the pitcher may have a little more or less on the ball or possibly even something new.* What's so important here is realizing and remembering the important relation between your observations and your timing. It's an *observation* followed by a *preparation*.

While we're on the subject, it's also important to realize that timing, and therefore observations, are personal. Just because *you* offset X amount of weight for a particular pitch doesn't mean that *I should as well.* Timing is established individually by talent. If you and I were exactly the same, except you were just a bit quicker, you would offset more weight on any given pitch than I because, due to your added quickness, you could allow the ball to travel closer to you before you would have to reach your balance point. Theoretically, you would be potentially the better hitter because you would have the ability to watch the ball longer than I. These two hitters can be seen in Diagram 23. Here, Hitter A, the quicker of the two, has a longer and slower pendulum motion, resulting in a balance point that arrives later than the balance point of Hitter B. Again, this results in the ball traveling closer to him before he must react. *He has more time.* Hitter B, on the other hand, has a shorter and faster pendulum motion simply because this hitter must reach his balance point sooner if he is to react in time.

Timing can also become individual due to the *quality* of a hitter's mechanics. Again, if our talents were equal but I pre-extended, lunged, or constantly started my stride late (it could be any number of mechanical breakdowns), I would time pitches differently than you. Much like Hitter B, I would need a balance point that arrives just a bit earlier than yours and therefore I would be forced to constantly commit my swing earlier. *Due to subordinate mechanics, I would be restraining my talents.*

If the individualism of timing is molded by both talent and mechanical quality, you should also be aware of another interesting fact. Even if you and I had the same *visual ability*, it would not necessarily mean that we were seeing the ball the same. Our eyes are judging speed only in *relation to our personal reaction ability.* A hitter's ability to see the ball the best he can is formulated by vision, talent, and mechanical quality. Did Ted Williams have the greatest eyes in baseball? *Probably not!* Did he have the greatest combination? *I wouldn't doubt it.* With this in mind, whenever you ask a fellow player about the speed of a pitch, have him compare it to another pitch and/or pitcher. You should do this because answers like *"He's fast,"* or *"He's slow,"* may be way off base through *your* eyes. Always gain that sort of information by *comparison.*

When you have a feel for offsetting weight properly, the only other ingredients required for good timing are *starting the stride on time* and *receiving the pitch you anticipated.* I call these three elements the *timing triangle,* which is no more than a simple model that hopefully will remind hitters what it takes to be on time. This model can be seen in Diagram 24.

23

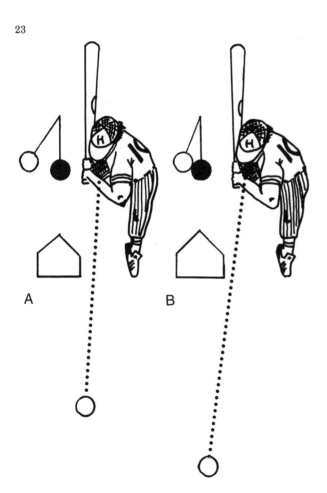

A   B

24

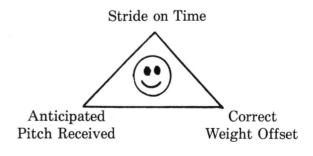

Stride on Time

Anticipated Pitch Received

Correct Weight Offset

This simple model, "The Timing Triangle", is merely a reminder of what it takes to be on time.

Obviously, each positive triangle — each correct offset of weight — will cover a certain range of pitch speeds that you can handle fluently. I mean, you don't have two separate triangles for 90 and 91 miles per hour. There's a *span* here, and though I am not sure at this point the size of this span, it exists and you must realize that. For learning purposes, if we imagine the span to be 9 miles per hour, what I'm claiming is that an offset of weight geared ideally for 85 miles per hour will cover any speed slower or faster than 85 miles per hour up to a 4 miles per hour *range* in *either* direction. Therefore, an offset of weight ideally for 85 miles per hour will cover the range of 81 to 89 miles per hour. This can be seen in Diagram 25.

25

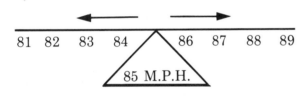

85 M.P.H.

Now that you understand timing, you can understand why it's always better to be early rather than late with your stride. When you're late, assuming you've gotten what you anticipated, you never reach the balance point in time. You don't land properly and you've got no hip action — no swing! But if your stride's a bit early you'll still get to the balance point, and you'll still be a *loaded gun*. I mean, you can still swing hard because your *legs* are in good position. One should note, however, that if you're *too early* your body will come to a stop, therefore eliminating the *headstart* advantages of your stride.

Timing Feel

It is now also easier to understand the clue of *timing feel*. Timing feel is just *realizing* from the flight of the ball if you're getting the speed you anticipated. Timing feel simply tells you if you're timing is *on* or *off*. Your timing feel provides any one of three different feelings, all of which have different meanings: 1) it can feel *good* when you've timed and guessed the speed well; 2) it can feel like you're way *early* when you get a pitch traveling *slower* than expected; and 3) it can feel like you're dead *late* when you get a pitch that's faster than you expected. Ya, I know at this point that sounds like common sense, but remember, the ball is on it's way; and when we're talking about three different pitches traveling at three different speeds, *common sense takes place in a split second*. A good hitter must be able to recognize how he feels and know immediately what to do from that point. Hey, if you've got less than two strikes on you and here comes a pitch right down the pipe, but your timing feel is telling you you're late, you should *take* that pitch; but many hitters will go right after that ball and stupidly pop it up simply because they don't understand or utilize the importance of timing feel.

You know, ever since you've been little, a good ball has solely been described by location — a good pitch was over the plate about crotch high. But as you go on that changes. It is my feeling that *timing outweighs location*. Provided the hitter has the right bat in his hands, an untimed pitch will do him in much quicker than a timed pitch in a tough location. This is why I have suggested conceding *location* when you're outmatched by a real tough pitcher. It's only sensible to cling to your timing because you have your balance and your stride momentum. Sure, we want good location too, but to concede timing for location, like the hitter I just described, is asinine. Good hitters use their timing feel effectively. If they *don't* get what they're looking for they *don't* swing. If their timing feel reads early or late they shut themselves off; the message is *No — no swing*. On the other hand, if the timing feel reads good then they'll continue to sort additional information (location, color, spin), which *may or may not* render a swing.

Now, I said earlier that timing feel was your main clue in identifying a pitch, and though that is true the *majority* of the time, I must admit that it is not necessarily true all of the time. Different pitches *can* travel at the same basic speed, and in sight of both this fact and the importance of timing, I feel it's better to think of timing feel as *the main clue that tells a hitter he does not want to swing.*

If you think about it, timing is where all the pieces start coming together. I mean, up until now you've been creating *time* and *strength* through good mechanical execution and now, through observation and calculation, you're bringing the advantages you've created to the point (in relation to a given pitch) where they can be used most effectively. *The hitter's ultimate ongoing goal is putting his time and strength on time through the alliance of his mental and physical preparation.* It is here where the *entire hitter* is tested, and it is here where most of the beauty and pain of the skill are encountered.

The Stride's Length and Height

Stride length also deserves some thought. How far should you stride? Is it two inches? Six inches? Two feet? Many times I hear coaches claim that good hitters have short strides and while I basically agree, I feel the topic contains some blanks to be filled. For example, what exactly are we measuring? And most important, how do you find the correct stride length for you? As far as I'm concerned, the length of the stride is the distance that the stride *heel* has traveled on the *heel line* from the stance. This distance is seen in Diagram 26. Although the toe has *rotated* much further, one should be concerned with the movement that brings the hitter to *balance*. This movement is the forward movement of the pendulum and is best measured by the stride heel's progression.

The length of your stride is *individual* and

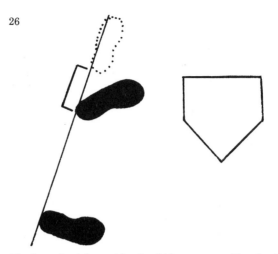

26

The length of the stride should be measured by the front "heel's" progression on the heel line.

will depend upon both the length of your legs and your flexibility. The best way to find stride length is to ask yourself this question: "Is my stride bringing me to my balance point with my legs *positioned properly*?" ("Is my front leg landing toe first, front knee still bent? Is my back leg still bent as it was in the cocking motion?") If the answer is "Yes," you have found good stride length. I have found that good leg positioning usually drops the stride at a distance *less than* the length of the hitter's foot. For example, my foot is 11½ inches long and I stride about 6 to 7 inches. Most of the little league kids I've worked with, having an average foot length of 7 inches long, had strides of about 3 inches.

As you might suspect, stride length problems are: 1) reaching out with the front knee; or 2) straightening out the back leg. If either of these movements occur during the stride, the stride's distance will increase, causing the hitter to land in a poor position for good hip rotation. The effect of these tendencies can be seen in Photos 53a and b. Again, when striding properly, the only lower body movement is at the hip joint.

Very rarely does anybody address the height of the stride, but it is also important. I believe in a *low* stride. In the outfield grass this stride would remain in touch with the grass throughout the entire movement. I like a low stride because, until the stride leg lands, the hitter is missing 50 percent of his swing. Remember, that leg represents *half your power, half your speed*; and without that leg *on the ground,*

53a   53b

If the front or back knee extends prematurely, the stride will be lengthened and a poor landing position will result.

you've got nothing. Why would anybody want to prolong its flight by lifting it up higher — bringing it further from its critical destination? I have found *high* striding many times to be a hitter's solution to his fear of striding on time. When you lift the stride leg *up*, your *body* really isn't going anywhere; the hitter is trying to move without making any commitment — *he's trying to move and remain safe.* High striding is no more than a camouflaged late or delayed stride; and again, if anything, we'd rather be early.

Furthermore, when a hitter lifts his stride leg higher than a few inches, he many times will *tilt* his shoulders back as seen in Photo 53c. This results in the landing of an *unbalanced body*, an overloaded back leg, and the loss of hip action.

53c

As staged, high strides are usually late strides that result in landing unbalanced.

Timing And The Strike Zone

Let's take a closer look at the term *contact area*. Your contact area is a *three-dimensional area*. It is as high and as wide as your strike zone, with a *depth* that is measured by the distance between its two most extreme contact points. These points, the high inside strike and the low outside strike, can be seen in photos 54a and 54b, while photo 54c illustrates the contact area's depth.

54a

54a and 54b outline the contact area extremes, while 54c displays its entire depth.

54b

54c

Your contact area holds a specific position in relation to both your *body* and the *pitcher's release point*. Holding off on the singles hitter, in Diagram 27 we see the relation between style, the pitcher's release point and the position of the contact area. Due to the *slightly closed stance* of the middleman he will contact all his pitches further from the pitcher's release point. This hitter's *stance* and *stride* have moved his entire contact area back toward the catcher, therefore providing him with the extra time we spoke of earlier.

Also in this diagram it is important to note that while the contact area can be moved in relation to the pitcher by stance and stride, it should not move in relation to the hitter's body. In both styles the outside and low pitch is being contacted at a point or depth about *perpendicular* to the *instep* of the front foot, while the high inside strike is being hit out in *front* of the body.

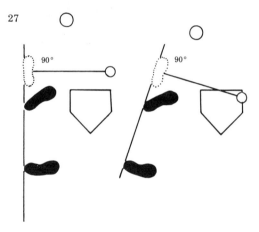

27

To hit the locations of the strike zone consistently and with authority, the hitter must strive to hit each location at its own specific *depth* in the contact area. Though a difficult task, the ongoing attempt to meet the different locations properly will help to build and maintain a consistent *mechanical and visual* approach to the entire strike zone. When a hitter neglects to hit his strike zone locations at their respective points, he is changing his swing! He is adopting new mechanics to handle certain locations; and this is a "no-no." For example, many hitters when facing an outside strike, for one reason or another, will come forward (*lunge*) as opposed to *waiting* for it and hitting it correctly at its proper depth. By altering their mechanics these hitters have changed their *swing speeds* and therefore their *visual combination. Remember, the quality of your mechanical execution effects how you see.* These hitters are using two different swings and two different viewpoints. As you might guess, these hitters experience their share of timing problems because two of their hitting constants, swing speed and vision, are now changing with location.

Okay, so you hit different locations at different depths, but how do you get the bat to them properly and at what depths are the different locations hit? The bat is brought to different depths of the contact area by rotating the hips to a *suiting degree.* Through a closer look at our contact area extremes, we can see not only the relation of *hip rotation to the different contact points,* but also the relation between the different *strike zone locations* and their *contact area depth.* As you can see in Photo 54a, the *high inside* strike is not only the pitch that will be contacted closest to the pitcher, but it is also the pitch that requires the most movement — the *greatest* amount of hip rotation. Due to the length of the rotation and the location of contact in relation to the pitcher's release point, up and in leaves the hitter with the *least* amount of time. Keep in mind, however, that due to the momentum created, this area is hit the *hardest.* On the other hand, *low and away* is just the opposite. It is contacted furthest from the pitcher, it requires the *least* amount of rotation, and therefore provides the hitter with the *greatest* amount of time. However, due to a lack of momentum, this area is hit the weakest. This can be seen in Photo 54b.

With the characteristics of the extreme locations in mind, take a look at Diagram 28. Here you see a strike zone surrounded by numbers, numbers that are *increasing* in value when traveling up or in; and *decreasing* when traveling down or away. After finding and adding the height and width numbers from any location in the strike zone, we have ourselves a number that represents two things: 1) the *reaction intensity* of the swing — the amount of hip rotation necessary to reach the contact point; and 2) the placement of a strike zone location to a specific *depth* in the contact area. For example, Pitch A on this diagram, with a height of 11 and width of 6, has the *high* reac-

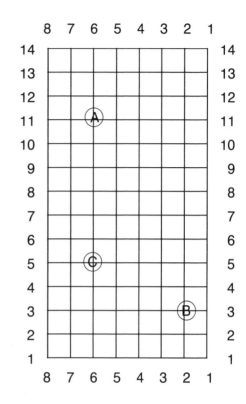

tion intensity of 17 (*22 and 2 are the extremes*). Shifting to Diagram 29, we see a scale that converts reaction intensity to a depth in the contact area. And in this case, due to the high

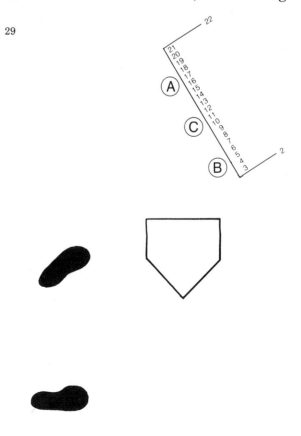

reaction intensity of 17, Point A is contacted fairly *early* on the scale (*closer to the pitcher*). Conversely, Point B, with a height of 3 and a width of 2, has a *low* reaction intensity of 5 and therefore, because it requires less hip action, it is contacted *later* or deeper on the scale (*further from the pitcher*). Point C, which has a reaction intensity of 11 (an intensity exactly between our high of 17 and low of 5), will be contacted at a depth exactly between the two within the contact area as well.

By creating this numbered strike zone I have designed a model to help the student bridge and understand the three-dimensional relation between his hip rotation, the different strike zone locations, and the depth in which those locations *must* be met for mechanical consistency.

A closer look reveals the fact that regardless of *strike zone location*, if the reaction intensity numbers are equal in value, they will be hit at the *same depth, with the same amount of hip action*. For example, in Diagram 30, though Points D and E are in separate strike zone locations, they will be hit at the same depth in the contact area.

A step further, in Diagram 31, I have divided your field area into three separate zones. These zones have then been labeled with a range of reaction intensities. The idea is to show (with less than two strikes) where the different strike zone locations should be hit *on the field* when executing with good mechanics (*the feedback you get from understanding where different pitch locations should be hit on the field is a must for the creation and consistent use of a sound swing*).

Below, regardless of strike zone location, if the reaction intensity numbers are equal in value, they will be hit at the same depth with the same amount of hip rotation.

30

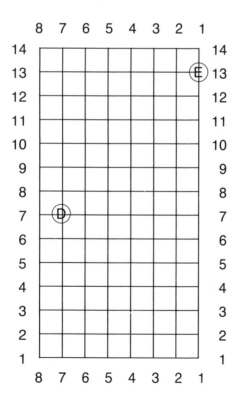

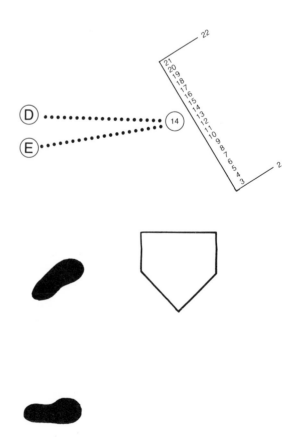

31

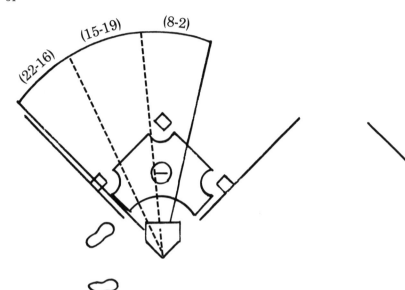

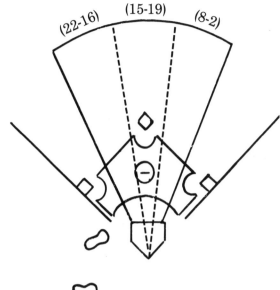

Here, we see where the different reaction intensities should be hit onto the field. Understanding where the different strike zone locations should be hit is a feed back must.

Starting the Swing: Trigger Timing

After understanding where, when, and how different locations are contacted, you can easily understand that although two pitches are traveling at the same *speed,* a difference in *location* may change their speed when viewed through the eyes of reaction intensity. For example, in Diagram 32, although Pitches A and B are both traveling at 85 miles per hour, Pitch A has a reaction intensity of 14, while Pitch B only has a reaction intensity of 6. Pitch A is a faster pitch due to its *location and contact point.* Because the majority of locations are contacted at different depths, the strike zone possesses a slight timing of its own — *a location timing that can and should be understood.*

When a hitter establishes a familiarity with the strike zone's timing, he is then ready to reap the benefits of what I call trigger timing. Now, trigger timing is no more than *starting your swing — pulling the trigger or popping the hips at the right time in relation to the* *ball's location.* After a timing feel that reads *on time,* and if the pitch is in the general area desired (boxes), the hitter will then continue to read and swing in relation to where the ball is located. Trigger timing is timing's *fine tuning* stage. It can be the difference between good and fair contact. I mean, if the ball's in the anticipated area and your pre-swing has placed your balance point on time, you *should* make contact. However, if you want to start converting a greater percentage of hit balls into screamers, you must start to understand and deal with timing on its fine tuning stage. For example, let's say the count is one-and-one and you're looking for a fast ball, even area; sure enough, your timing feel reads good and here it comes; but it's on the *low outside* corner of your even area. Many hitters not having an understanding of what's going on will be a hair quick on that ball and ground it out (*when your "early" with a slight up-swing, you will hit the "top of the ball — on the other hand, if your "late" you'll hit the "bottom").* But the hitter that understands the timing within his strike zone knows that that pitch is really a bit slower, and therefore he will delay his commitment just a hair and have a better chance on it. How is this done?

82

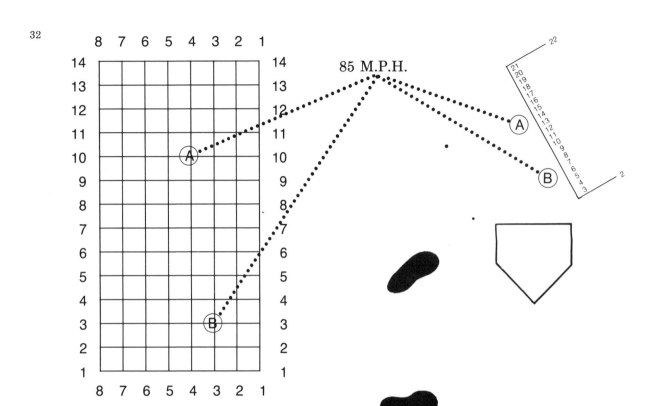

D32 shows how two 85 mile per hour pitches are really traveling at different speeds when viewed through the eyes of reaction intensity. The hitter that understands this will be at a great advantage.

Mechanically, there is no preparation. Trigger timing is just seeing, knowing, and reacting from a well-timed balance point. After a good timing feel and when the ball is in the general area you anticipated, you will continue receiving even more information that will confirm the pitch's location in more detail. At this point, much like timing feel, you will receive one of three messages: 1) right on the nose; 2) a hair late; or 3) a hair early.

Naturally, if you're on the nose, you would then just go ahead and swing. However, in this case please note that these feelings of late or early are only *slight*; and therefore at this point the hitter is just slightly on either the *ground ball or fly ball side of a line drive.* I want you to realize that because he is only a *hair* off, the hitter now possesses the ability to *adjust physically.* Therefore, if you're late, you just drive the hips hard and catch up. While, if you're early, you delay and then explode. In both cases we are thinking about being *quick with the hips*, quick enough to get the fat part of the bat on the ball. *Of the two feelings, early is the most brutal because you have to keep watching and then attack. It's hard to call off the dogs — to fight from pulling the trigger.*

Unlike the stride, with trigger timing you would much rather be *late* than *early*. When you're early, a mistake is headed for the end of the bat and rolling wrists. However, when you're late, you've still got a large and solid hitting surface to hit with. *Though it's better to be "early" with your stride, it is far better to be "late" with your swing.*

Now, I realize that catching up or delaying sound like tough tasks, and you may think I'm getting too complicated with all this talk of timing, but I'm not. With good mechanics, you won't believe how much information you can absorb and react to. *Don't sell yourself short!* When you're on time with your balance point, catching up and waiting become entirely possible. When you're balance point is on time, you can *make* things happen.

Now, trigger timing becomes more difficult as the anticipated area or box is enlarged — the larger the area, the more balls and timings you must deal with. For example, Points A, B, C, and D, marking the *rip area* in Diagram 34, have reaction intensities of 19, 15, 11, and

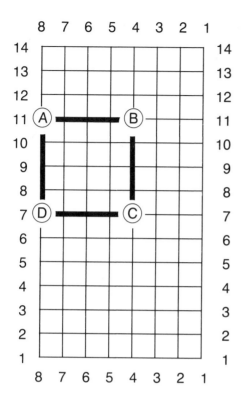

34

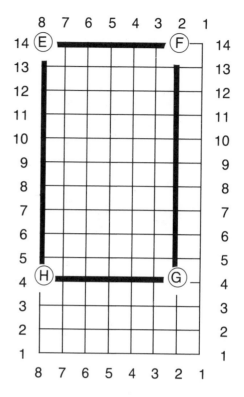

35

15, averaging out to an overall rip area intensity of 14 (the average being the dead center of the area). Comparing the *average* intensity to the *highest* and *lowest* possible points of that area, 19 and 11, we find a fluctuation of five notches (14+5=19 and 5+9=14). Now, Points E, F, G, and H of Diagram 35 mark an *even area* in the same size strike zone, but have reaction intensities of 22, 16, 6, and 12. While their *average* also comes out to be about 14, the *highest* and *lowest* possible intensity points of this area, 22 and 6, are 8 notches from the average, an increase of 3 notches or a location icrease of over 50 percent (14+8=22 and 8+6=14). This increase of pitches to be timed can also be seen in Diagram 36. Here, the *third dimension* of each area comes to life.

With this in mind, I want to point out that when looking for a pitch in a specific box, we always look for that pitch in the middle of that box. We want to work from the center — the average, because from there it is easier to get to the extreme locations if necessary. For example, on an anticipated even area pitch, I'm preparing for a speed in the middle of that box as seen in Diagram 37. If I were thinking

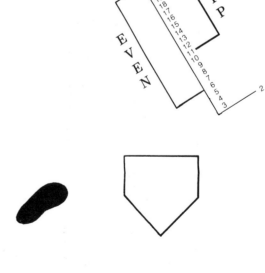

36

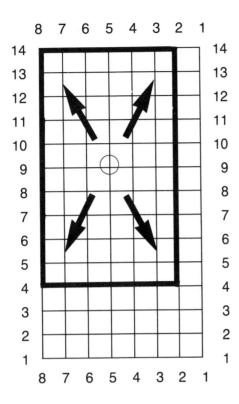

When anticipating a pitch in a certain tunneling area, we want to look for that pitch in the "middle" of that area. Here, we play the average of that area, making it easy to adjust if need be.

of something low, there would be much more catching up to do on the high extreme as seen in Diagram 38. Again, we're playing the average.

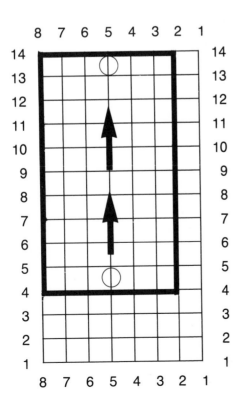

Other Strokes

The Inside Out Stroke

The inside-out stroke is a shorter swing designed for contact. Its qualities make it not only the ideal swing for the *singles hitter*, but also for any hitter with *two strikes* or facing a *slump*. By setting the hitter's contact area *further back* in relation to his *body* (as seen in Photo 55), the inside-out stroke enhances contact percentages by simply providing the hitter with more decision time.

Its main mechanical difference is that the arms and wrists *never fully extend*. This in turn creates a shorter swing, a *swing with a lessened range of motion*, making the hitter not only *quicker* but more *accurate*. By not extending the arms and wrists fully the bat will now *trail* or be parallel to the hands at contact.

55

Because the arms and wrists are bent the bat will now contact the strike zone locations from a *new angle*. Due to this, our previous relationship between where the ball is located in the strike zone and where it will be hit onto the field *changes*. The balls will now be hit to the *plate side of the heel line*. Now it is as if the army tank is shooting just slightly to the *right* on a right-handed batter (Diagram 39).

39

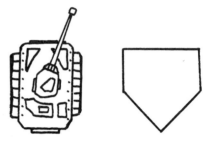

Due to the position of the arms and wrists at contact, when using the inside—out stroke, balls will be hit to the plate side of the heel line. The tank nozzle is now slightly to the plate side.

With Two Strikes

How is the inside-out stroke used with two strikes? When a hitter finds himself with two strikes the fight for time becomes *amplified*. Not only is the hitter facing his largest area (the entire strike zone), but he also must now *sacrifice the aid of guessing*. To combat these problems the hitter must be able to react as quickly as possible. Therefore, when a hitter gets his second strike, several other adjustments should be made along with the use of the inside-out stroke. The hitter should: *1) level off his bat; 2) choke up, or even better, switch bats to a lighter model with an identical length; 3) move closer to the plate and deepen the stance in the batter's box; 4) concentrate on hitting the ball up the middle — that is, hitting the ball in the same area that the middleman does normally; and 5) most important of all, open up the stance and stride.*

Now you may give me flack for recommending an open stance, but think about it. What is the *main adjustment* in making a stroke quicker and shorter? It's a *reduction in hip rotation.* The more rotation, the longer the stroke; the longer the stroke, the more time you need to bring the barrel to contact. With two strikes, we want to *shorten the distance between the barrel of the bat and the contact point.* This is done best by opening the stance slightly before we even start. One should also note that because the ball is directed *away* from the hitter with the inside-out stroke, opening up also becomes a *necessity* for hitting the ball up the *middle.* These adjustments can be seen in Photos 56a, b, and c.

56a displays the two strike adjustments: leveled bat, back foot closer, deeper in the box, hitting up the middle and an open stance.

56a

56b

56c

56b and 56c relay two strike contact on the inside and outside corners.

The Singles Hitter

Understanding the inside-out stroke, you can see why the singles hitter, the true runner, should always use it. Remember, his most significant physical talent is his *foot speed,* and he would be crazy to jeopardize not making

contact as consistently with a longer stroke. Hitting the ball harder but contacting it less is not in the best interest of his ability, especially when he's on the turf.

With two strikes, the singles hitter simply remains in his originally slightly-opened stance. The singles hitter, executing the inside-out stroke properly, gets to the ball quicker than the other two styles. He does not need to shorten his stroke. Also, due to the nature of his style, the singles hitter will not face as many two-strike situations. Again, the tendency is for pitchers to go right at them. Resultingly, the singles hitter must guard against being over-aggressive.

Interesting to note is that in a sense, *all styles* become *singles hitters* with two strikes. All styles must *concede* to the pitcher with a stroke geared toward *quick, solid contact to all strike zone locations. Now I said earlier that when a hitter gets two strikes, he doesn't guess, and he can't. There's no taking a pitch with a wrong guess now. Your back is to the dugout. Therefore, when a hitter receives two strikes, he must prepare his pre-swing for the pitcher's mid-speed pitch.* That is to say, if a guy has three pitches, one traveling at 60 mph, one at 70 mph, and one at 80 mph, you'd prepare for the 70 mph pitch because that timing makes either of the other two pitches easier to get to. With two strikes we are coming to the balance point at a time that will enable us to adjust to the pitcher's extremes (one should note that this sort of adjusting can only occur successfully with the two-strike swing). If the pitcher doesn't have a mid-speed pitch, the hitter *pictures* the speed of a pitch that would be traveling between the two extreme speeds and prepares for that speed. For example, if the pitcher had a fast ball that traveled at about 80 mph and a curve ball at 60 mph, you'd imagine and prepare for a pitch at 70 mph.

In closing, a hitter should note that *the quality of a hitter's technique will rest on his two-strike execution.* Solid two-strike hitting enables a hitter to be confident and selective before two strikes. A hitter that is afraid to be under the gun has the tendency to open up his *rip and even areas* early in the count, when he could be taking his chances on the next pitch, *reaching potential demands good two-strike execution.*

On the other side of the coin, when you do master the inside-out stroke and feel its rewards, don't sell your soul to the devil of average. If you have the ability to blast balls, don't cut your potential short and hang out with the inside-out swing. Use your talents to reach your style's potential. I hate guys who wimp out on their style. Leave singles hitting to legitimate singles hitters. Do the work and display this skill and your ability with dignity.

Opposite Field Hitting

What about going to the opposite field to move runners? For this I recommend using what Ted called his left field stride. Here Ted both *backed off* the plate and *closed off* his stance. Then, using his arms as described with the inside-out stroke, he would stride *into the ball* (like a middleman normally would) and direct it to left field. This can be seen in Photo 57 as a right hander.

57

Much like Ted, when your job is to go to the opposite field I recommend that all styles *close off just slightly*. However, I don't believe the average hitter must close off as much as Ted did. When trying to go the other way, *again the slight pre-extension of Ted's top arm*, forced him to close off a bit more. After striding, Ted's back toe would line up with his front heel. You, however, should not have to close off any more than the slightly closed stance I described for the middleman. These degrees can be seen in Diagram 40. Also, keep

40

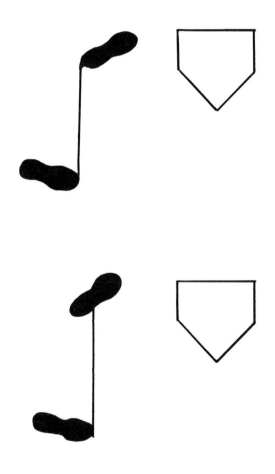

Though displayed with right handed hitters, this diagram shows the angle of the Williams opposite field stride and what I feel it should be with the arms executing properly.

in mind that you may not have to back off the plate. While it's true that Ted backed off it's important to realize that many times he was doing it to beat the Boudreau shift (the Boudreau shift was a defensive maneuver that stacked the third baseman, shortstop, and center fielder on the right side of the diamond where Ted was known to hit the ball, hoping he would hit into the shift Ted was pitched *inside*). *Naturally, by backing off the plate it became easier for him to deal with this new crop of inside pitches.* What I'm getting at is the fact that most players are *not* facing shifts, and therefore standing off the plate may *not* be to your advantage. For example, if you're a powerful middleman with a man on first, facing a normal defense, and the hit and run sign, your ability to hit the long ball may cause the battery to pitch you away. Naturally, if you're off the plate like Ted was you'll be forced to *reach*. A hitter's distance from the plate in an opposite field situation depends on how the pitcher has pitched him in the past.

Opposite field hitting reminds me of something else worthy of discussion. Ted talked about *closing off* as a way to gain time, claiming that when you close off your stance you keep setting your contact points further from the pitcher's release point. Naturally, I agree. We've already talked about that. Many times however, I'm asked why I don't advocate hitters closing off their stance with two strikes. Why not go to the opposite field more so than up the middle? Though the *opposite field swing* can provide an increase in decision time, it can *not* bring the hitter to *all* strike zone locations effectively. Try this. Position yourself in the box so that you can reach the *outside corner* with inside out arm execution and the opposite field stride. Do you think you can hit the *inside pitch*? I can't. The inside pitch becomes murder, while *inside and low* becomes next to impossible. With *two strikes* we've got to set up in such a way that will cover *all locations.* It just can't be done as well with the opposite field stroke.

Mechanically speaking the reason is that the *angle of the stride* clashes with the *deepened contact area.* Remember, regardless of the type of swing you're using, the hips have got to *lead the way*. They've got to clear out for the arms and bat! When standing at a distance that would enable you to reach the outside

corner and supposedly all pitches from there in, my point comes to life. When positioned like this, the hitter seems to *run out of hip rotation before the bat can reach the inside* contact points. The result is an upper body swing with a loss of speed and power. Think about it, if we want to reach further, be quicker, and clear the hips, we have got to get *closer and shorten the swing* and this can be done best by moving closer and opening up.

I know, now you're going to argue that Ted Williams used the opposite field stroke with two strikes. I'm not going to argue with that. I'm sure he did. But he had good reason to. First and foremost the *short left field wall at Fenway,* and equally in his favor his reputation as a *power pull hitter*. When Ted wasn't facing the shift, I'd bet he *did not back off the plate* because *without* the shift the tendency was to keep it *away* from him. Without the shift Ted's *pull with power* reputation *decreased* the amount of inside two-strike pitches he faced, therefore enabling him to go the other way with something on it.

Did Ted play it smart? Sure, as a matter of fact it's a great example of *individual style,* however, it is individual! When it's Ted Williams at Fenway Park — great! But on the average, most hitters would be losing out adopting that sort of two-strike leverage. The opposite field stroke is longer, it takes more time, and therefore, again, it's not as accurate as the two-strike position I've suggested. Closing off also starts the barrel of the bat further from contact, and I'll tell you something else, with two strikes I don't like the angle on which it brings the bat's barrel into contact. Opened up you'll have more bat surface to hit with and more bat in the contact area for a longer period of time.

Hitting to all Fields

We've all heard about hitters that hit to all fields, and it has become something that young hitters look up to and often strive for. Personally, I feel it's one of the *worst* things you can do. There are two popular methods of spray hitting. After increasing the depth of the contact area, *a characteristic they both share*, the first approach attempts to *pull the inside pitch and punch the outside ball the other way*. In some conversations this approach will also feature a stride that steps in the direction of the pitch after the pitch is in flight. That is, *"in" for the outside pitch and "out" for the inside pitch*. Unfortunately, this is *extremely difficult*, due to the deepened contact area the hitter has *too many locations to time and recognize*, not to mention the body quickness needed to get inside or the lack of hip action caused by the late stride.

The second approach tends to be more popular; here the hitter, again with an extended contact area, attempts to split the plate in half, trying to *pull* the inside half of the plate with a *normal stroke* and *inside-out* the outside half with the inside-out stroke. Not only does this hitter have to deal with the extra locations and the timings of them, but he also must decide in a *flash* how he's going to use his *arms* and *wrists*. Naturally, he has his share of hassles. First off, he usually draws a blank on the *central locations* because he can't decide quickly enough how to approach them — how to use his arms. And even worse, this hitter, much like the hitter I described earlier, is seeing the ball through the eyes of *two techniques*. This type of *seeing* shatters any chance of quality *information storage*.

In my opinion, hitters that attempt hitting to all fields never hit as well as they could have — it's too hard! Forget it. If you see hitters as I do, that hit to all fields with success, you should keep in mind that they could be far better if they were to hit within the boundaries of their style.

A Few Anticipated Questions

Pinch Hitting

This section highlights the answers to a few questions that I feel you may be inclined to ask; for example, how can you take a pitch you haven't seen if you're pinch-hitting or when they change pitchers on you in the fifth? This is a good question because many times these situations are tight situations, and I agree that often you *cannot afford* to take a pitch for information purposes. So what do you do? Well, the answer really depends on what you have done in the *past*; again, not just on that day, but in previous meetings. Regardless of whether you're in the game or not, the good hitter will be doing his homework and remembering his past assignments. When you've done your homework, weighing and measuring the situation at hand will be much easier, and the observant hitter will have no problem formulating his idea of a good ball for this type of an at bat. Again, it all comes down to how you're going to play the at bat; and naturally, the more alert you've been, the more accurate your decision will be. Depending upon the pitcher's talent, you may decide to take a peek at one; or on the other hand, you may decide to go after the first ball if it meets your requirements. If you've never faced the pitcher before *(depending upon the game situation)*, you might want to use your two-strike swing throughout the entire at bat.

The bottom line is *information*; and a good hitter steals and remembers every piece of information in sight. Whether he is pinch-hitting or facing a reliever, the good hitter will always have an information edge.

Controlled Headstart

There are also a couple of points in reference to stride. First off, I said stride was a *controlled headstart*, and I want to expand on that because often hitters don't understand that the stride is only a *part* of the swing. *Just because a hitter strides on time, he shouldn't feel obligated to swing.* What makes the stride a controlled headstart is the fact that only the *legs* can start the swing — the rotation of the hips. The stride and the swing are really two separate phases of the puzzle. It's a stride and then a decision to swing that *"looks like"* one smooth motion.

Also, you should note that both guessing and good timing technique will eliminate a hitter's fear of striding on time and build confidence. Learning the tie between guessing and timing is a great day for any hitter because he'll experience the consistent advantage of being *on time* for every anticipated pitch. After this experience, the hitter usually finds himself despising any late strides while his confidence starts saying things like, "I can hit that now." *Proper use of guessing and timing can bring a hitter a long way in a short time.*

Stride Off Motion

I'll tell you something else; often after hearing my spiel on timing, someone will question; "Why not forget about bending the back leg for different offsettings of weight and fluctuate the balance point by starting the stride at *different points* of the pitcher's delivery (diagram 41)?" Why not? Well,

41

Some people believe that the stride will start at different points in the pitcher's motion for different velocities, I disagree.

although that sounds like a logical idea, it's impossible because the pitcher's arm is traveling much too fast for you to see and remember different starting times. These people are talking about three different speed pitches, all having different starting times, recognized by watching an object moving fast, 60 feet away. The speed of the pitcher's arm, plus the *angle* in which you would be trying to identify these starting times makes this idea impossible, *The hand is quicker than the eye.* While we're in the neighborhood I must confess that in actuality strides for different pitches *do in fact* end up starting at different points in the pitcher's motion. However, this is accomplished by the offsetting of the different weights in the cocking motion. Though you will *feel* as though your strides are starting at the same time, in reality by bending the back leg more, and increasing the *backward flow* of the pendulum, you will slightly delay the stride (the forward movement) and resultingly delay the arrival of the balance point.

What I want you to realize is that this task can only be accomplished by *feeling* the different weight shifts and starting at a time in the pitcher's motion that can be easily recognized, which is, *before the high speed extension from the throwing arm's elbow* joint.

Drawing A Line

This reminds me of something else I want to say. Throughout this book I have tried very hard to speak in simple terms about something very complex. Hitting is not an easy subject to talk or write about. It reminds me of algebra, every thing building and depending on its previous steps. What I'm getting at is that a few times I have skipped a detailed explanation and presented the concept in a way that I felt it could be basically *understood* and *experienced* the quickest. For example; earlier when talking about the stride I said that different offsettings of weight would cause you to *fall forward faster or slower*. Well, that is not really *true*, (all things fall at 32 feet per second), however, it certainly *feels* as though you're falling faster or slower and therefore explaining it in that way makes it easier for the hitter to grasp. I also said that the *legs* control hip rotation and that is not entirely true either. Much of the hip rotation is caused by the *abdominals* rotating the *pelvis* on the *femur*. What I want you to realize is that when you do something like this, you have to draw a line. I decided the best route was to get the information to the right people in a form that would be read, understood and debated.

Rhythm

What about movement in the stance — *rhythm*? Lau called it an *"absolute,"* claiming that all hitters move a bit in the box. Whether it's a flapping Joe Morgan elbow or a wagging Carl Yaztremski bat, good hitters move while they wait. He then suggested that hitters should rock in their stance just slightly from foot to foot to comfort themselves and get themselves ready — a kind of idling effect. Well, I used to believe it. I used to teach it. I experimented with it for three years; and my conclusion is that rhythm (movement before your pre-swing) is a personal issue. *I view rhythm as a way of dealing with tension and not a mechanic.* Now, don't get me wrong. If you want to rock, go ahead; it can work, but it's hard to teach a young kid because it throws off his stride timing. Mechanically speaking, your pre-swing will provide all the preliminary movement you need to swing. You don't have to move before the cocking motion unless you feel a need to.

Early Bat Movement

Often I'm asked about starting the bat's movement in the stretch position; that is, to begin the bat's arc as you create the stretch position (before a swing decision). This movement is displayed in Photo Sequence 59a-d. Ted did this, and it can definitely be advantageous because it gets the bat moving early; and it seems to prime the arms' movement. It also gets some momentum going back, which ends up decreasing the amount of weight that must be offset in the cocking motion on any given pitch. But, it can be tricky to learn and maintain because when the bat comes *down*, the movement must be from the *wrists*. The arms (forearms and upper arms) should still remain in the basic position they held in the stance. What gets tricky is

59a   Cocking   59b   Stretch

59c   Mid-Stride   59d   Landing

the fact that when this is done correctly, the top hand wrist tends to *bind back uncomfortably*, and the tendency becomes to raise the front shoulder to relieve the discomfort, which places the body in an unbalanced position when it lands. Like I said, it could be an advantage, but I need more time with it. I thought I'd throw it out for you to think about as well. While I may seem to be leaning towards this idea, there is another part of me that wonders whether or not it might be best for the bat to be leveled off right in the stance as in 59d.

The Feet

The movements of the feet are also a wonder in the hitting world. I feel Sequences 60 and 61 explain the movements of both feet efficiently.

60a

60b

As the front leg extends, the front foot heel swings under, the foot then rolls over with the follow through.

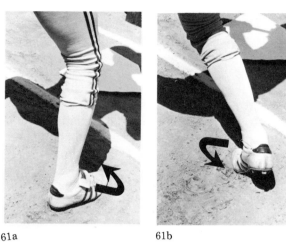

61a   61b

Here, the back foot rotates on its ball. With the weight favoring the little toe side of the foot in the follow through.

60c

61c

Moving The Areas

What if you have a high rip area as I do and the pitcher convinces you that he's going to keep it at the knees all day long? Should you take two low strikes? No. In this case I would move my feet further apart, bend my knees more and mentally lower the rip and even areas. By doing this, again, we have favored *timing* over *location*. *A hitter can hit an anticipated pitch in a tough area much better than he can hit whatever comes with two strikes.* Remember, with two strikes, guessing, our number one timing resource, has been sacrificed.

On the contrary, what if you've got a low rip area and a pitcher proves to be consistently upstairs? Do the opposite. Higher your rip and even areas, but please understand in both these cases I'm talking about a pitcher *you know*. This isn't a decision you make after three batters. Don't get carried away with this. Use it only against pitchers who demand its use.

Another .400 Hitter

Do I think there will be another .400 hitter? You bet there will be; he's way behind schedule. There are more guys that could hit .400 in the pro game today...forget it, I don't want to talk about it. It won't be long.

Little League Mom

My turn. Do *you* know who could really help this skill? The little league mother! I'm serious. I've found many mothers to be miles ahead of their husbands in the *logic department*. Do you know why? Because they're working from scratch. They don't have a bad hitting background; and as a result, they don't try to mold their kids to be only what they were. Certainly, there's something to be said for their lack of ego. I think this is an ideal

94

opportunity for mom to be more than a fan or a source of transportation. Hey, if mom can read and reason, she can help. I've seen it before.

I'll tell you something else, I think many times at a young age a kid has better lines of communication with their mother; and I don't think they feel as pressured around her either. Now, I'm not saying that she'll throw good B.P., but she can definitely help this skill; and I hope she tries.

Individual Style

What about the refined part of style; individual style? After a hitter begins to utilize good technique through a suiting basic style, he is then ready to start finding and developing his individual style. When I think of individual style, I think of it as the last staircase leading to a hitter's potential. I mean, once he's got the basics down and is directing his main strengths and weaknesses through his basic style, the next step is a fine tuning process — a focus on the hitter's *subtle* strengths and weaknesses. Individual style asks the question, What *personal adjustments* must I make to bring my ability and technique to potential?

Now, subtle may not be the best word to describe some of the adjustments I'm referring to because they are very important. For example, *mechanically*, individual style covers issues like; distance from the plate, bat selection, location of both the rip and middle areas, pitch selection (type of pitch), rhythm and offsetting weight. While, *mentally*, it looks at; all phases of hitting preparation, attitude, practice routine and dealing with pressure. Individual style also runs into the *psychological* part of the hitter; analyzing quirks, superstitions and fears. Physically, mentally and psychologically, these things add up.

Identifying individual style is a trial and error period, where the hitter takes a detailed look at himself and exactly how he hits. The hitter in search of individual style keeps his *basics sharp*, while he consistantly asks, "Is this right for me? Would I be better off doing this?" This search takes time, it is literally years of observation and analyzation.

Today, very few hitters get to this stage

from a solid base. If you do, however, keep in mind that *reaching potential* and *maintaining* it are two different things. Because individual style is based on *you*, it can *always change*. Years later you might find yourself asking individual style questions once again; "Too much Italian cooking, Joe? Getting smarter? Too confident? Who are you *now* and how should you hit for the best results?

Softball

I know many will want to know about fast pitch softball and from what I've seen of it, I would say that everything would be the same except for the plane of the swing. I've seen games where the ball has come in *level and I've seen games where it is consistently coming up*. While the name of the game is to match the plane of the bat with the plane of the ball, I can't say I would have all my

Former Hanover High School star and University of Massachusetts/Amherst hopeful, Mara Frattasio anticipates a pitch.

hitter's swing down against a ball that was coming up. The reason I say this is because that would make the *ideal hit* a ball contacting the infield at a depth just behind the pitcher. I don't think I'd want all my hitters hitting the ground *before* the infielders. If you're a singles hitter — sure thing — meet the plane — swing down. But I don't want my first baseman, who has taken a strong liking to peanut butter cups, hitting consistent grounders. I'd rather have her swing level and sacrifice some contact percentage in return for a ball hit within the boundaries of her *style*. With two strikes however, she would then swing down and hit up the middle.

Front Foot Angle

Earlier I talked about how the front foot toe should *not* "turn back" with the front knee in the *cocking motion*. While I felt it would be confusing to expound at that point, now I feel you can fully understand that if the front leg swings to far *back* it will *delay* the hitter from reaching the stretch position at the proper time causing his bat to be late. Red Sox right fielder Dwight Evans does this right in his stance and it kills him. Photo 62 displays this position.

I Don't Guess

Sometimes I'm asked about the good hitters who claim in the media that they don't guess. I usually answer by asking; who controls a hitter's salary? When most answer the club owner, I disagree. The people who pay a hitter are the people who pitch to him and therefore I would call you naieve if you think a guy making a million dollars a year is going to tell *Sports Illustrated* and *every pitcher in his league that he guesses*. The obvious thing to do is to claim you *do not*. If pitchers are stupid enough to believe that, then they'll really think you're good and as a result challenge you more often with their best pitch. This in turn makes guessing much easier.

62

Here, I am dispalying a front foot that has rotated back with the front knee. This will lead to a lagging swing.

Too Hard Now

Due to the player's comfort and confidence in his past approach, I know many coaches may feel that applying this theory at the professional, college or high school level may be too difficult. With the pressure and learning environments of these levels in mind I can't argue that point. *This book may well be more effective at the lower levels of baseball.* However, please don't get me wrong. That is not to say that the information presented here is sub pro, college or high school, respecting Ted's work as its' mother, I don't think anyone else has gone to this extent. Certainly, I'm not saying hitters *can not* improve while playing at these levels, but the decline in overall technique, statistics and therefore success has prompted an immature and uneducated attitude toward teaching and practicing this skill.

While I am more than confident that good instruction can improve hitters on any of these levels (Washington Senators, 1968); realistically I know good instruction will not be present. I guess what I'm saying is if you want to be good, you must be someone that *has* or *will make* the time to do so. If not, chances are you'll face *an extended growing pain period* at the higher levels.

Cross Coaching

What if you start making progress with this theory and your coach crosses you up? That is, he wants you to swing down. Well there are two main characteristics I've found in most coaches; 1) they all have egos, and 2) they love to win. What this boils down to is that if you advertise the fact that you're taking pride in a *new hitting approach, other than what they have shown you,* they may be offended and they will surely make note of it. Sure enough with the first sign of failure — you'll hear about it.

On the other hand, the tendency is to leave well enough alone; therefore, if you're doing well with *what ever you're doing* you'll probably be in the clear. If your coach is closed minded, I advise keeping a very low profile. However, if your coach is sincerely open minded, tell him what you're trying to do and *why.* You may be putting a state championship in his ear.

Momentum

Sometimes, when I talk about *the two strike position,* someone will argue that a 200 lb. Steve Ferroli can use this shortened stroke and still have the *power* to hit the ball with authority; however, the 150 lb. short stop can't get the ball past the pitcher with that stroke. Well, when coaches use the word *power* in hitting they really mean "momentum" (*a mass times a velocity*) and what I want hitter's to understand is that many times that 150 lb. short stop has the ability to generate every bit as much *momentum* or *power* as the 200 lb. hitter. What I'm saying is that if the quick fast running short stop is swinging his 150 lbs. at 100 m.p.h. while the 200 lb. hitter is swinging his weight at 75 m.p.h. they have created an *equal amount of momentum.* What

happens today is that the quick light hitters get lured away from using *their bodies* at an early age. They're taught to use their *arms* to hit and their *legs* to run, when they should be using their *legs to hit and then their legs again to run.* Obviously, this applies to all swings not just the two strike swing.

Why Up The Middle With Two

Why hit the ball up the middle with two strikes? Well, first and foremost, when hitting up the middle you have a greater chance of making contact because the bat is in the potential contact area for a longer period of time than in both the pull or opposite field strokes. Looking at the field, its middle is the *largest area* because most times center field is much deeper, and there are *zero* well hit foul balls! There is also a wide spectrum of difficult plays for not only the short stop and second baseman, but, also the pitcher. Using the shortened two strike swing I've suggested, all hitters *can* and *must* reap these advantages.

Follow Through

Everybody talks about the follow-through, and to avoid being to much of a radical, I've included these photos. Notice how the body has completely rotated with the feet flopped over. If you do everything right before this phase, chances are your follow through will be camera ready.

What about the Charlie Lau — let go of the bat follow through? *Because the Lau theory brings the hitter's weight onto the front leg with a planted and closed front foot, the hitter runs out of hip rotation early.* This, for comfort's sake, *forces* the hitter to let go of the bat with the top arm. (*This arm cannot reach to where his body wants to bring the bat.*) Not only do I think this is foolishness, I also think these hitters look like they should be playing in the woods with Christopher Robins to the tune of a flute player dressed happily in tights with a belled cap.

Light Bats

You've probably been thinking that Ted Williams was a great supporter of *light bats,* and that I'm going against him. Well, I think Ted was a strong advocate of the *right bat,* and that's important. I think Ted felt you should have the lightest bat that can do the job, and I feel the same way. But remember, *outside pitches are part of the job, too.* If you asked me, "Did Ted Williams use a light bat," my answer would be, "No." The way I see it, for his ability, "The Splendid Splinter" used

a *good bat,* a *smart bat.* Hey, most of the homerun hitters around Williams at that time were more compact compared to Ted; and in comparison to their bats, I'm sure Ted's was extremely light. But the word, *light,* can only really be defined in the eyes of your ability and mechanical execution. Also, if you've read it, his section on bats in "The Science of Hitting" is entitled, "Light but right."

Figured Out

Often, someone will ask what if the pitchers know the areas you like and keep their pitches away from them; should you take two strikes? No. That's when it gets to be fun because *now you can look for location as well.* Hey, they used to pitch Ted *away* with *sliders,* a location and pitch he didn't care for, and he had a field day with it because any time you can predict both the *pitch* and *location* your timing should be next to perfect. What could be more fun?

Even Stance For Kids

I said the majority of hitters are *middle men* and they are, but when teaching a young boy (ages 9-12) I always set them up as pull hitters. I do this because the straight stride aids them in clearing the hips. They'll have plenty of time to adjust when they get older and have a better understanding of how the strike zone is approached.

Head Moves Back

Some people ask me if I think the head moves back during the swing. I think it does. You can see this back in 22a and 22b. Sometimes I'm questioned whether this effects what I see. No. Again, after a swing decision, my eyes are starting toward the field of the anticipated hit. You know with the head coming back I feel I save time. It's like going away for a football pass as opposed to coming in for one.

From a marked starting point, these two photos show the difference of head movement between the Lau and Williams theory from a different angle.

Early Stretch

Sometimes, I'm asked why not just start in the stretch position? Sparing the details, you'll be quicker if you put the *to be used* muscles *on stretch* just an instant before the task. It has to do with an elastic type characteristic of muscle fiber.

3 and 1

Many times I'm asked about the 3 and 1 count. If you've prepared for a fastball in the rip area and you get a fast ball for a strike, out of that area, should you swing or should you take it and go 3 and 2? Well, it depends on the pitcher and the game situation. If the pitcher's tough, you might want to extend to the even area. On the other hand, if he's "cake" stay in the rip area and go to 3 and 2. If you need the long ball, and you're the man to do it, you might want to take a shot at the 3 and 1 pitch if it's not in a bad spot. Remember, to hit consistently with two strikes, you've got to sacrifice power.

Too Weak

What if a kid isn't strong enough to swing the proper bat? Well, then he works at getting strong enough so he can! We don't make a *technical adjustment,* I mean we shouldn't say okay, use a light bat and reach. This kid is no different than the kid who can't dribble left handed — he's got to do the *work* to get there. In the meantime, without broadcasting it, he'll just have to sacrifice the outside corner using something he can handle correctly.

Goof Ups

Closing off this section, you're right, I did take some of these pictures with the label facing up and yes, in some photos the ball is hanging on a string. You should have seen my friend Kenny holding the fishing rod . . . I hope you're this observant in a game.

Practice

Another factor that makes hitting so hard is practicing it correctly. To practice correctly, you a need a list of things; you need a pitcher or a machine, decent baseballs, bats, a mound, a decent backstop and playable weather. And unfortunately, even if you've got all these things, often it's still not enough. For example: *the pitcher has got to throw at the speed you'll be seeing and with control.* You can't practice when only every fifth pitch is a strike or if you're constantly worried about getting drilled. What about all those holes in the batter's box? You can't practice when the local box has two 5 inch cleat holes the size of a bread box. Those holes can cause a hitter to stand and stride off balance. They can also dictate your style for a day by forcing you to trade the angle of your stance and stride in return for some stability. The box should be level, and that's important. We can't forget the cost of baseballs; or even worse, losing them. You go down to the field (if there is one) with that one friend who never says, "No," and you start throwing to one another; and before you know it, you've got balls going everywhere. You know what I mean; it's like they're trying to escape. Good baseballs are expensive. *You've got to have a mound*; that's imperative. *If you throw off level ground, the ball will approach the hitter on a different angle, drastically distorting your feedback.* A flyout on flat ground may be a line shot off a mound. Don't forget that. How about the weather? You can't use baseballs in the wet; you need something that won't pick up the water. I have found those hard machine balls with the stitches to work best, but you still need someone to throw them. (You can't use a machine in the rain). Naturally, nobody will throw in the rain — rain is a throwing repellant! Whether it's pitching batting practice, or just throwing in general, when it rains and/or the temperature drops a bit, it seems like everybody is haunted with the fear of a potential arm injury. You'd think everybody was under a multimillion dollar contract — too much care; not enough dare. It's really kind of funny watching a high school player who can't field a fly ball to save his mother's life, shift into a protective and reluctant attitude with the first sign of rain. What puppies.

When and if you finally get everything right, the big question is how do you practice. Well, if you're a mature hitter — if you can swing, guess and make corrections, I recommend live practice — as much as possible; that is, *a pitcher throwing off a mound, outdoors and to a catcher with a live and normal count — not 1-and-1, but 0-and-0.* While practising, the hitter should pay strict attention to where and how the ball is being hit in relation to both where the pitch was in the strike zone and how much weight he had to offset in his pre-swing. Also, the hitter should question any call made by the catcher (catcher umpires) that didn't seem correct from his point of view. Remember, the catcher has a better viewpoint, and a hitter can use his observations to help him understand exactly where pitches are crossing the plate.

In a live practice session, the pitcher *must be trying* to get the hitter out. This is why I like to see live practice in a *competitive atmosphere.* The *mature hitter* should always practice under pressure. This is where I think betting is great. Bet against your buddies for a pizza. If money is a problem, bet on situps or sprints. When there's something to lose, you'll try harder. There's pressure in a game; and I feel a mature hitter must practice not just his hitting, but his hitting as he deals with pressure. If you take the pressure out of a mature hitter's practice, you won't be doing him any favors.

I have no doubt that live hitting is the best form of practice, because live hitting is the closest thing to actually hitting — it's mental and physical execution under pressure. However, when teaching a *young hitter,* a little leaguer or even a pony leaguer at an age where the fast ball is obviously the dominant pitch, *the physical outweighs the mental.* At this age the majority of boys are better off with some good hitting drills as their prime form of practice while live hitting falls secondary. The only reason I say this is because a *kid won't give a hoot about getting the good ball, walking, style or two-strike hitting until he is confident he can hit the ball hard*; and at that age, that stems from a decent, well-timed swing. Also, once the kid learns to swing, the mental aspects become easier to teach because, again, he'll see the ball better.

These drills that dominate a young hitter's practice are not just for the young hitter; they also keep the mature hitter physically and mentally in tune; and if you don't already know it, a swing is something that must be *maintained*. Sure it gets easier to maintain as you climb towards perfection; however, I don't believe any hitter ever gets to the point where he outgrows his swing maintenance. What are these drills? Well, certainly, we've got to stride on time; and this comes down to simply timing different pitcher's motions. Games on TV are great; it's just the pre-swing over and over. You think fast ball on one; curve on the next. You practice offsetting different weights and starting on time. You can also have a friend make-believe pitch to you. The more motions you time, the better off you'll be.

The *direction* of the stride *must* be correct. This can be practiced by drawing your heel line in the dirt, and then after striding, looking down and checking where you've landed. A piece of athletic tape on the floor is good, or even better, a straight low wall, like the picnic bench seen in Photo 63 or even a curbstone. By striding the stride heel along the wall, the hitter is forced to land his foot in a decent position.

I'm also big on *mirror work* because you can see yourself. I feel hitters should check their swings from different angles and at different speeds; sometimes freezing and then observing. Are you apart in the stretch position? Is that front foot staying put during the cocking motion? How's that front arm — pre-extending? Am I balanced in my stance? Hey, mirrors are for telling you what you look like — use them. If you don't have a full-length mirror, large store windows are great, but, keep your distance...

A good hip rotation drill can be executed by pausing after you land in the stretch position; and then while concentrating hard on the timimg of the leg movements, the hitter pops his hips through, striving for speed and fluency. After awhile, the leg movements will jell, and the hitter will feel very natural with his hip rotation. If, however, a hitter can't time these leg movements himself, I recommed moving the legs manually for him. In Photos 64a-d, you can see how I'm pushing the front knee in, while spinning the back foot. Now the hitter *feels* himself falling into the dip phase, and most times can duplicate that movement after a short time.

63

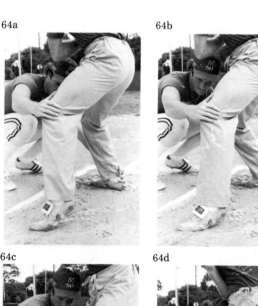

64a

64b

64c

64d

102

Proper hip rotation should account for a swing where the head remains in place, or just slightly behind the starting point. You can check for this two different ways; first by lining your head up in your stance with something across the plate that is perpendicular with your shoulders. *After* you swing, you look back to that point, making sure your head and therefore body have not *come forward.* This can also be done with a rock placed on the ground in the *shadow* of your *head.* With your *back* to the sun; again you swing, making sure the rock stays in your head's shadow.

Another drill I've designed for hip rotation I call, *fall backs.* Here the hitter goes through his pre-swing and swing. However, at the beginning of hip rotation, (the dip phase) the hitter brings his back foot totally off the ground, causing him, if he's executing properly, to thrust straight back and down, where a partner catches his fall. This drill trains the hitter to use that front leg *with power,* and also allows him to feel the back hip fly forward freely. This drill also helps the hitter to feel the slight upswing plane and how his body can achieve it. Photos 65a and b show this drill.

his hands move forward, the tension increases; and the hitter must fight to maintain its bent position. This setup can be seen in Photos 66a-b. Another good drill to prevent pre-extension; is swinging close to a wall, as seen in Photos 67a and b. Here the hitter is forced to keep his arms bent correctly or he'll hit the wall.

66a

66b

67a

67b

Photos 65a and 65b display a drill for hip rotation that keys on training the front leg for power. While above, we see two drills for bringing the arms into contact correctly.

65a

65b

How do you learn to *anchor* that front arm? After cutting a bicycle inner tube and tying one end to something stable, the hitter will take the other end in his hand, and with a bit of tension right in his stance, he will begin to slowly move through his pre-swing and swing. Naturally, as he falls into the dip phase and

To assure unbroken wrists at contact, driving into a rolled up rug, car tire or football dummy as seen in photo 68a is excellent. The hitter has got to feel resistance. In fact, I believe a young hitter should never practice his swing without hitting something for resistance. The rolling wrist epidemic is too probable. This is why I view batting tees, the soft toss drill, whiffle ball or hitting tennis balls as bad practice. *Any time there is minimal resistance at contact, the hitter can hit the ball more comfortably with rolling wrists.* When the ball has no resistance, kids will practice incorrectly to succeed in a drill that has little to do with hitting. It's crazy, and I see it everywhere — at all levels.

I'm not real down on whiffle ball; I just view it as advanced. Once you understand how a ball is contacted, whiffle ball can be great for the *mental aspects* of the skill. You can make a whiffle ball talk, (Thurman Munsen ball) and the pitches are much better than in baseball — real sharp off-the-table breaks; and you don't need a lot of talent to throw a sharp breaking ball. Whiffle ball is like live practice, and it can be good; however, I know it can cause rolling wrists as well. Hey, everything in life depends.

Another great supply of resistance, as well as a teaching aide, is hitting a dead basketball When teaching young hitters, I have found great success with this technique because if the hitter does not meet the basketball correctly, it will hurt. Once proper contact is mastered, I then progress to smaller objects, like volleyballs, a rolled-up tarp or water-logged softballs until the hitter can consistently execute properly with a baseball. Remember, timing contact with a baseball can be difficult; and by *increasing* the size of the target, you help the hitter time and contact the target correctly, allowing him to feel, learn

and understand the unbroken wrist concept.

One of my favorite drills is one I use for getting the head out. Photo 69 shows me in my backyard hitting a snowball; and you can see my head is out. Naturally, the reason my head is out is because if I had put it *down* to hit the snowball, I would have gotten a face full of snow. You learn quick! For those who aren't fortunate enough to have snow... a rolled and soaked towel will also get the job done. I know you think it's funny, but, hitting snowballs can be good practice. Hey, after you hit a snowball, snow will stick on the bat, showing you exactly where the ball was hit. Plus, there can be decent resistance from a snowball if it's real heavy snow. Snowballs could be New England's answer to winter B.P.

69

Above, hitting snowballs can be good for getting the head out. Also, note the balls on the fence that I took. Though you can't curve a snowball, you can change it's speed and have tunneling and guessing battles with a friend.

68a   68b

Another good drill is what I call *"beeming"*, and it's great because it's mental and physical. In Photos 71a and b you see a sheet about 15 feet away from the hitter. What you do here is have your friend stand with a flash light to the side of the sheet while you go through your pre-swing, anticipating a certain pitch. Naturally, your friend can tell by your pre-swing what pitch you're anticipating, and he has the ability to shine the flashlight behind the sheet at any time and at any location. If it's the right pitch in the right place, then go ahead and pull the trigger, blasting down the dummy with unbroken wrists. As you can see, the sheet has both curve ball and fast ball tunneling zones. I don't recommend playing with more than two pitches because the timing on the pitcher's part to beem can be tricky, but two different speeds are easy and it's fun. You can strike each other out looking, get each other to chase bad balls; it's great practice and you can do it almost anywhere. The advantage to this drill is the fact that it keys on the hitter's *tunneling and guessing*, while really zeroing in on his *timing feel*. If the pitcher or beemer wishes to give the hitter the speed he has anticipated, he merely snaps the flashlight on when the hitter's stride foot hits the ground. Any time the light is on before that, the pitch will be much quicker than anticipated, while the light going on after that point will make the pitch much slower. In this drill the pitcher's wind-up is imagined; however, with a third player, you can put the wind-up in on the side.

Many times players and coaches ask me for a practice program, but I don't feel I'm able to design a program because I feel it's personal. I know if I were coaching a major league team, I would have all my players practicing on individual programs from the stretching right through to the sprints. Everybody would be doing something geared toward improving their personal weaknesses. I certainly would have all my hitters using all the drills I described; however, the percentages of each drill would depend upon the hitter. *Ideally, a hitter should practice what he's weak on without letting his strong points slip.* Again, it comes down to a self-evaluation. You've got to answer questions honestly, and that can be hard. Don't let pride camouflage weaknesses; get them out in the

71a

71b

This is what I call "beeming". It is an indoor drill that keys on tunneling, guessing, and timing feel.

open, (at least to yourself) and design your program around them. If you doubt your judgment, ask a friend; "Do I look good on the curve? Do you think I'm a decent two-strike hitter?" Shop around for answers, but don't ask fools.

There are a few other odds and ends that deserve your attention, for example, *slow pitching.* Any time you practice against slow pitching, you're headed for both pre-extension and rolling wrists. You're better off bunting that crap. Slow pitching provides very little resistance, plus it's increased arc distorts your tunneling — distorts how you see and read *good pitching.* Fast pitching is much better; it's pitching like you're going to see, and it's pitching that *demands* good mental and physical execution for success.

I don't like donuts and weighted bats either because they *bend reality.* When I go to the plate, I want to know the exact weight I've got to swing. I don't want to think I'm quicker than I am. I want to know exactly how quick I've got to be and exactly the weight I've got to do it with. Yah, maybe there's a psychological advantage there because the bat feels like it's lighter, but it's not, and that's what I don't like. As far as the off-season goes, weighted bats may be okay; but now we're talking about using the weights to strengthen yourself rather than to fool yourself.

While we're in the neighborhood of on-deck warm-up, I feel the on-deck hitter should not only watch the pitcher and the pitches thrown, but warm up by finding or reassuring the timing of his pre-swing, and taking "check swings." If a hitter can hit something that offers resistance, that's even better. I laugh when I see these guys whipping the bat all over the place — all hands, arms and follow-through because they're only hurting themselves. Stay away from that nonsense. On deck it's a short tight swing — just to an assumed contact point.

I can't say enough about hitting *outside* as opposed to *inside* because the background distances are totally different. The *figure and back ground relationship* makes these settings two different worlds. It's much harder to hit outside. Also, if you're in a cage, you lose the feedback of how hard the ball was hit, its flight and where it would have landed. Naturally, if you've got no other means, cages are great,

but try to get some time outside before the season gets too close or you could be surprised.

People always ask me about machines, and I like to talk to them about them because they can be dangerous to your mechanics. Most of the machines I've seen throw *consistently,* but they don't allow for the hitter's pre-swing — they don't let him start his stride early — *anticipate.* Instead, they fire the ball out at you like it's coming out of a gun. *They cause you to be late and usually lead to poor arm and hip execution from a catch-up type of swinging.* I like the *arm machines* because you can see the arm and anticipate. Master Pitching Machine makes a great arm machine. I haven't seen a better one. The tire machines can be O.K. as long as they have a long enough ramp for the ball to roll down.

It's also important for the machine to be at the proper *height.* It's a must to have the balls coming *down* because again, any time the pitch plane changes, your feedback will become distorted. You've got to shoot the right balls as well. If you use real baseballs or the plastic balls with stitches, the balls will move randomly; they'll tend to die, run and flutter. I don't recommend that type of practice; it's too inconsistent and it can be dangerous. Those *hard dimple balls* are best; they are aerodynamic, like a golf ball, and they pitch straight and consistently.

I also recommend a *wooden bat* when practicing because they're true. You'll feel a bad-hit ball on a wooden bat, and I think that feedback is valuable. Also, you can swing a wooden bat hundreds of times without chewing your hands to ribbons. The aluminum bats have rubber handles, and they will wear your hands away to nothing — some taped handles are even worse.

As far as batting gloves, pine tar and the whole grip-tight market, experiment with them; it really depends on where you live and you. However, if you're in the cold, I'd definitely wear batting gloves.

I highly recommend weight training as well. I've heard Ted say many times that he wishes he had done more; but I'd be careful with the upper body — with the shoulders and arms. Remember, you've got to throw the ball as well. I'd go power from the waist down, with heavy weights, at three to eight reps; and with light weight from the waist up, 15 to 20 reps.

Make sure you're lifting these weights properly. A bad lift with heavy weight could cost you — be smart.

I'm also big on flexibility; good flexibility will enhance ability and decrease injury percentages. Stretch out good always.

If you don't have access to weights, use your noggin. I mean, put your brother on your shoulders for squats and toe raises, squeeze a rubber ball; certainly, pull-ups, pushups and sit-ups are easy enough; and bicycle tire tubes can be hooked up for a number of resistance exercises. Don't sit back — make things happen. When you do pushups, however, I recommend you do some of them as follows. Photos 72a and b show something I designed called *hitter's pushups*. Note how the right arm, the top arm, is close to the body; while the left arm, the bottom arm is perpendicular to the upper body. Also, notice how the power arm palm is facing ahead, while the lead arm palm is facing back. These pushups cater more to the *arm muscles involved in the swing*. If you have trouble at first, I recommend that you start out doing these pushups on your knees and then progress to your feet.

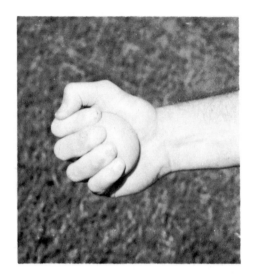

Squeezing a rubber ball can be good for forearm strength.

72a

72b

Photos 72a and 72b display what I call hitter's pushups. While my brother, Mark, provides a "lift" in a makeshift workout.

Finally, the *attitude and philosophy* surrounding the practices of any hitter are geared toward improvement. It's not recreation; it's more of a school setting — an educational setting. And just like school, practice can be the most *fun you've ever had or it can be hell.* Hey, if you do well, you feel great; but you try to recognize the reasons behind your success and learn. On the contrary, if you stink, you feel lousy, but you still try to recognize why and learn. *Again, we see the need to observe and analyze.*

Now, I've talked about attitude, but a good attitude will only go as far as the *motivation* that fuels it. *You've got to get yourself interested. You've got to use your imagination.* For example, if my team is losing by 10, I literally talk myself into the fact that we're only up by one; this keeps me sharp when the tendency is to go through the motions. Williams spoke of motivating himself with *goals — realistic goals* and I think that's great. Goals also keep you sharp. If you happen to be down ten in the ninth and you come up with one out; sure, it looks dismal, but you don't pack it in for the day. Instead, you say "I'm going to get a good ball and get a hit because my goal is to hit .310 this year." Goals are simply another form of motivation.

There are many forms of motivation, and *you know* what gets *you* going. I wish I had a buck for every time I announced my own major league at bat — or a friend's for that matter. Nothing was better than singing the National Anthem on the sidelines with Billy and Scott and then charging out onto the field for a hundred flys. Movies can get you all fired up. I do complete scenes from several Clint Eastwood movies. Certainly, I don't have to mention books and music. Hey, your attitude is fueled by what you see and hear, so use that to your advantage.

Trouble Shooting

This short section is designed to help you find the *problem*. Again, the good hitter must be able to make the proper *corrections and adjustments*; he must have a feel for *self-coaching*. Here I have listed five common hitting problems and the areas where their cause is most probable:

I. Swinging late, getting jammed and popping up:

    A.   Are you striding at the right time?

    B.   Are you getting in the stretch position?

    C.   Is the bat too heavy?

    D.   Are you using your arms properly?

    E.   Are you bending the back leg too much in the cocking motion for the anticipated pitch? (Offsetting too much weight)

    F.   Are you losing the angle of the front foot in the cocking motion?

    G.   Are you rotating the back foot?

    H.   Are you just hitting the bottom of the ball as opposed to the middle?

    I.   Are you launching the swing from a balanced landing?

II. Lunging:

    A.   Are you keeping the back leg bent when you stride and land?

    B.   Are you letting the front knee continue to bend after you land?

    C.   Are you getting in the stretch position?

    D.   Are you striding too far?

    E.   Are you reaching that front knee out rather than landing it bent with the leg in a fixed position?

III. No power but making contact:

    A.   Are you rolling your wrists?

    B.   Are you getting in the stretch position?

    C.   Are you launching your hips from a balanced landing?

    D.   Do you have a firm grip?

    E   Is there give in the shoulders?

IV. Early, grounding out:

    A.   Are you striding too early?

    B.   Are you preparing well for the anticipated speed?

    C.   Are you gripping the bat correctly?

    D.   Is the bottom arm getting up and out of the way?

    E.   Are you rolling your wrists at contact?

    F.   Are you hitting the top of the ball as opposed to the middle of the ball?

V. Doing everything right and not hitting the ball as hard as often:

    A.   Are you getting the *good pitch* to hit?

    B.   Are you stealing all information possible from the pitcher?

    C.   Are you making the proper changes for two-strike pitches?

    D.   Are you preparing for the probable speeds correctly in the cocking motion?

Book Review

Rod Carew "The Art and Science of Hitting"

What I'm going to do here is assume you've read Rod's book and tell you what I think of its contents. I think it's important to stay up to date on all materials. Unfortunately, in this book, I've only had time for the most popular.

Starting with the *negative;* I don't like his statement about learning a little bit of hitting from different people. He claims there is no distinct path to hitting excellence and I think there is. He talks about *controlling* the confrontation between you and the pitcher, that is; do what you want to do, not what the pitcher wants you to do. I don't think of it as

taking charge or controlling, I think it's better said that the hitter must be able to *face the confrontation* — to *adjust* and *prepare* for it. Remember, the pitcher has got the ball and at the start of an at bat I think he *is in control.* I say this because if he's smart and talented enough to throw the right pitch, I won't swing. This, however, is very difficult for him to do consistently.

He advocates hitting to all fields. (I've disagreed).

Rod doesn't believe in waiting for good location and will even swing at a "ball" if he thinks he can make something good out of it. (I've disagreed)

Rod doesn't believe in *guessing.* He prepares for the fast ball and then gears down. (I've disagreed)

He never addresses the starting time of the stride and indicates on p38 that it starts after the ball is on its' way. He also claims for

AP/Wide World Photos

certain pitches that you should step "in" or "out", again, after the release. (I've disagreed with all of this)

He talks about landing the stride foot softly and I used to believe this as well, but I've come to realize that when you do this, you end up having to much weight on the back leg at the wrong time and it slows your swing down. You're not hitting from a balanced start.

He talks about bending the knees to get to the low ball, that is, to bring your body on its' plane. I don't like it, your eyes are dropping and it cuts your hip rotation. Bend your knees in your stance.

Many photos show him pre-extending which I'm strongly against. He also advocates resting back on the hind leg in your stance. I don't like this because you just come forward. There is no pendulum action. *When preparing for a certain speed pitch, it is very important that a forward flow starts smoothly immediately after the backward flow, like one*

complete motion. I should have amplified this point earlier. The other thing I don't like about it is, that, in your swing, the back leg has a very *stressful* job to do, why *fatigue* it in the stance?

Rod is a head down swinger who does not believe in the slight up swing. He claims it puts to many balls in the air. I've disagreed with both.

He talks about coming from the back foot to the front. However, his photos display movements that seem to walk a line between Williams' and Lau'. I think he is vague on this point along with how to use your arms.

Practicing, he likes batting tees and slow pitching and I don't like either.

On the positive side, I think the book says some great things about attitude, dreaming and confidence. Carew talks about how he pushed himself and how he wouldn't accept failure on a given pitch, I admire his attitude.

I like how he relates contact percentage to

proper mechanics and I love the statement about good hitting being a "campaign" — an all-out cause to work toward.

I think he made some solid points about what I call "style", and I like the term "altered state" when he talks about concentration in games and practice.

I like what he's said about selecting bats and using wooden bats in practice, and I agree that the stance is the *foundation* of your swing.

I thought he made some good points about reading pitchers, but, they were somewhat vague.

I loved the analogy between music and hitting movements on page 61. I think he made some fine points about stride length and its' consistency. He believes in *unbroken wrist* contact which he calls *flat hand* hitting. I like what he said about waiting for the breaking ball on page 75. Rod's comments on video as a teaching aid are great and I think (as he does), that all hitters must be willing to make mistakes in return for improvement.

Before we get into this conclusion phase please understand; I like Rod Carew! From what I've *read* of him, (I've also read his first book — *Carew*) I think he is an intelligent, hard working, talented athlete. I also like his sense of humor. (*Guess who's coming to dinner... I almost peed my pants.*) When I finished reading his books, however, I was saddened. It became clear to me that he had ended his career miles from his potential. I mean, here's a guy with a ton of attitude, smarts and talent approaching the skill *without* the *aids* of; guessing, correct stride timing, efficient arm execution or a *consistent* weight shift. (*I've seen many photos of Rod out in "front" and many of him "back", it comes from not guessing.*) In my opinion, Rod's success has been compiled by a *great attitude*, (again No. 1) and elite athletic ability. Remember, we are talking about a man who stole home plate 17 times — 7 in one season. We are also talking about a man (though he did not care to) who could hit the ball for power. Rod would tell you that himself.

Technically speaking, I think he was lacking in many areas. To me, he was doing it the hard way! He did choose the proper *basic style* for his ability which served him very well. In his book, he explains how he used the open stance that I've suggested for a singles hitter 80%

of the time.

Pete Rose on Hitting How to Hit Better Than Anybody

Again, like Carew's book, I will assume you have read Pete's work and tell you what I think of it. Starting with the negative; I don't like *associating comfortable with right,* Pete is big on comfort and I am all for it, as long as it remains within the boundaries of logic. For example; he believes in a comfortable grip and I've seen comfortable grips ruin hitters a hundred times (previously discussed).

Pete claims that fast hands are the key to hitting. I would say fast hips, arms and hands. Pete also claims that ideal contact is made out in front of the plate; that is not true for all hitters on all pitch locations. Pete believes in the level swing, again I've disagreed. Pete claims home run hitters have big looping swings. Home run hitters don't *have to have* big looping swings, but, certainly many have fallen prey to that tendency.

Pete likes the batting tee; and I'll tell you straight, if I could, I'd like to have a batting tee *bonfire.* Not just because it lures rolling wrists, but also, because you have to address the tee properly to insure good mechanics. That is to say, you have to understand where to *set your stance* in relation to where the ball is tee'd. Most people do not have that knowledge and would be much better off leaving that sort of figuring to their instincts while facing a moving pitch.

Pete also does not *guess,* much like Carew, he prepares for the *heat* and then *down shifts.* No thanks. He talks about guess hitters who strike out looking. Good guess hitters don't guess with two strikes. Pete feels guess hitters are less consistent. I think they're far more consistent. He talks about guess hitting as a home run hitters characteristic, I disagree. Guessing for any hitter is to increase hard contact percentage. He also watches the ball into the catcher's mitt if he doesn't swing. Don't do it. Leave your eyes out in front, let the ball go by and listen for the call. This will help you learn the strike zone from the proper view point.

I don't care for the terms *defensive* and *aggressive* hitter. He says be aggressive — even to the point of hitting pitches that are out of the strike zone. I see no percentage in swinging at a pitch that is not a strike. If you let it go by, you have increased the percentages that the next pitch will be a better one. You've also picked up more information. Sure, you'll hit bad balls well now and then, but, on average, you'll pay the pitcher. (You will have increased the difficulty of the skill by increasing the amount of pitches and timings that must be dealt with).

He does not talk about when to start the stride at all. Getting started is vital. Pete thinks a hit is most times better than a walk. I disagree. If you're "the man" in a tight situation, sure, open your areas and take your shot, but if you go outside the "gray area", you have probably cheated the hitter behind you. Chances are, he is a much better hitter than you, when you are swinging at a wide span of locations. Pete also says go to the *opposite field* to break a slump. I disagree. There is a greater contact percentage when trying to hit up the middle.

I thought his section on practicing was vague. At one point he talks against fast pitching in B.P. I disagree. He feels B.P. is to build confidence. I understand what he means, but that sort of confidence can disappear in a hurry when someone blows 3 by you on national television.

On the positive side; I agree that the changing of speeds makes hitting so difficult. I also think, as does Pete, that hitters should do their own job — play their own game. I like what he said about crouching because you'll see the ball longer, you're closer to the optimal angle of projection, and you'll decrease your strike zone size. The problem with crouching is that your legs must be very strong in order to support your weight consistently at the new knee angles.

Pete also believes in unbroken wrist contact and I like the fact that he starts his hands toward the top of the strike zone. (The place where you must be the quickest). Pete says the goal is to hit the ball as hard and as often as possible and I couldn't agree more. Contrary

to Lau's book, *Pete also feels George Brett is a back foot hitter* (page 50).

I love what he says about being patient and looking at what the pitcher has. He also looks at the first at bat as almost a *sacrifice*. He doesn't like first pitch hitters. (I'm assuming he just means first time at bat). Pete makes some positive statements about *knowing your self* at the plate — *style*. I like how he looks at striking out as something that happens. I also like how his *goal* is to hit the ball hard *regardless* of whether he gets on base. Line outs are jobs well done.

I like how he uses the marks on his bat for timing feed back, I've done that, and I know Ted did it as well. Pete relays what it takes in the attitude department very well. He is an all out player and I think that's the only way to do anything.

I think it is attitude that has created Pete Rose's success. Let's face it, the guy is a true American hero — the Bruce Springsteen of baseball. Technically speaking, (using his book as a reference), I would have to say that he also was a good distance from his potential. 1.) he didn't guess, 2.) he makes no reference to stride timing, and 3.) he did not hit out of the stretch position. (On page 49 he says; "As you bring your hands forward to meet the ball, keep your weight on your back foot as long as possible. Then, bring your front foot forward in a short stride of about eight to twelve inches.") Because the hands are moving before the front foot, he *can not* be in the stretch position. Looking at his build, I always wondered why he didn't hit the ball harder; now I know. The kicker is that he does hit it hard! He has 160 home runs or so, but if he hit with his entire body, as opposed to just his upper body, look out.

He also said on page 34 that he stands far off the plate and back in the box which is evidence of him being a pre-extended hitter, (previously discussed).

I know at this point you may be saying that I'm down on everybody, or maybe you're saying that Carew and Rose were great hitters and didn't do half the things my book says to do. Well hear this — for every Pete Rose or Rod Carew that has had the right combination of talent and luck to succeed in the major leagues, there are a million ballplayers looking up at them that need every edge they can get just to play at the high school level. These players aren't on your TV — you don't see their failures. I have, and knowing what I know I had to speak up. Hey, I'm not downing these guys, again, I'm just saying they did it the *hard way*.

The disadvantage that Carew and Rose have faced, (along with so many others), is that they have played the game in a low era of hitting technique. In a sense, they have been unknowingly trapped by the flow of baseball history from their potential. This bothers me. In hopes of clearing up what I've said here about talent, technique and the effect of the era, let me state this: if Rod Carew had approached the skill with the Williams' theory, (as a singles hitter), I think he would have hit the .425 mark somewhere in his career.

A Personal Note

For me, learning to hit correctly has been agony. By the time I read Ted's book I was 17 and I was under pressure; batting fourth in my high school lineup, being scouted both in high school and in the summer, off to college to battle for and hold a position — it was hard. When you're all alone, becoming a good hitter takes time; toss in the New England weather and time is just what I didn't have.

After reading Ted's book, it was obvious that the poor mechanics engraved in my swing since the little league level were limiting my performance; and suddenly I had a very big decision to make. I could either cling to the technique I had, trying to make the best of it; or, *while under the gun,* I could strive for fine technique with the *Science of Hitting.* Well, though I had a fine college career when measured against my peers, today looking back I know that in relation to my potential I wasn't even close. God only knows how many other guys experienced the same thing; not to mention the ones who quit, thinking they just didn't have it. It's sad.

I guess what hurts today is knowing that I can teach the average 13 year old to *"swing"* (not to hit, but to swing) as *sound* as Ted did in three weeks. That's assuming I see him four days a week for an hour a shot and he does the homework drills I prescribe. It took me *five years* to break bad habits — five years of *understanding and relearning.* Hey, coaching isn't everything, but it's close; and believe me, teaching a kid strong basics at an early age is the way to do it.

You know, it's funny; hitting a baseball has always been viewed as extremely difficult. And today, due to inferior approaches, it's viewed as being more difficult than ever. I totally disagree. Today a kid with good technique and decent athletic ability can do very well. *I've seen it teaching over and over again.* In a sense, the hitting decline has made this skill a skill of *opportunity.*

With all this in mind, my original dream continues to surface; that being a chance to hit in the major leagues — a chance to hit now that the pieces are in place. I feel my *come from nowhere success* would send up a flare

that would shine a great deal of light on the fact that hitting can be *improved.* Adding a sportman's twist, let me drop my gloves at center ice and say this; as a full time player, I'd bet the rights to this book that I could hit .280, (with power), in the first year, and .300 within the next two. No minor leagues. No seasoning. Right in, right now. When I say this however, please don't get me wrong, the intention here is not a chance for me to hit in the big leagues. My hope — my campaign, is merely for a *chance* to restore the quality of hitting and the level of baseball interest. And why? Because I believe baseball, and more specifically the skill of hitting, can provide millions of children and young adults with a reliable reflection of life's demands. By upgrading hitting's technique, I feel the game would not only be played longer, but also, more intelligently. I feel baseball's truest rewards would then be felt to a greater extent when those spikes finally claim their inevitable hook on an unsung wall of fame.

As for those who'll doubt me, I only ask these questions: have you tried what I've suggested and do you know what I know? I have traveled from poor technique to refined technique and retraveled that road again and again with a thousand students. I'm not saying anything new, "hitters aren't born; they're made!"

On the lighter side, I'm not an untouchable. If you've got a beef or a helpful comment, write to *Line Drive Publishing*. On a similar note, I'm planning an ongoing monthly publication called "The Hitter's Hot Line". This publication will answer questions and review hitting materials and equipment. If you'd like information please indicate this on the order form. I'm also planning on getting into the lecture world more regularly and I am also organizing several tours where I come into organizations and work with both the hitters and coaches. If something like this sounds appealing, again write to *Line Drive Publishing*.

I'm sure it won't surprise you when I say I love the skill of hitting. Due to both its trying physical and mental demands, for me, hitting has been a period of realization — a relatively safe place for me to learn about myself and the world around me. Think about it; it's all there; love, hate, jealously, ego, success, failure, trying, caring, reward, punishment, fear, courage and preparation. Ya, it's all there; and by dealing with it in hitting, I know the skill has helped me and will continue to help me throughout my life. No one knows it any better than I do; Hitting a baseball can be a great experience. If hitting to potential is your dream, I know this book can bring you there.

Order Form

For a copy of *"Disciple of a Master" (How to Hit a Baseball to Your Potential)*, please send $9.95 to:

Line Drive Publishing, 113 Pleasant Street, Hanover, MA 02339

Please include $1.50 for postage and handling and allow adequate time for delivery.

Name _____

Address _____

City _____ **State** _____ **Zip** _____

How did you hear about this book? _____

_____

Are you a coach or player?_____ At what level?_____

Would you be interested in the "Hitter's Hot Line"?_____

For a copy of *"Disciple of a Master" (How to Hit a Baseball to Your Potential)*, please send $9.95 to:

Line Drive Publishing, 113 Pleasant Street, Hanover, MA 02339

Please include $1.50 for postage and handling and allow adequate time for delivery.

Name _____

Address _____

City _____ **State** _____ **Zip** _____

How did you hear about this book? _____

_____

Are you a coach or player?_____ At what level?_____

Would you be interested in the "Hitter's Hot Line"?_____

"NOTES"

"NOTES"

"NOTES"

"NOTES"